Houghton
Mifflin
Harcourt

On Our Way to English®

Student Edition

Printed in the U.S.A.

ISBN 978-0-544-23533-5

9 10 2331 22 21 20
4500817719   A B C D E F G

ON YOUR WAY

You're on your way to English. Soon you will listen, speak, read, and write English as if you had been doing it your whole life! This book will get you there, and so will your teacher.

Be yourself. Tell others what you think about what you are learning. Invite them to share their thoughts with you, too.

Sometimes your classmates will help you. Sometimes you'll help them. Even though you come from different places, you are all on the same journey.

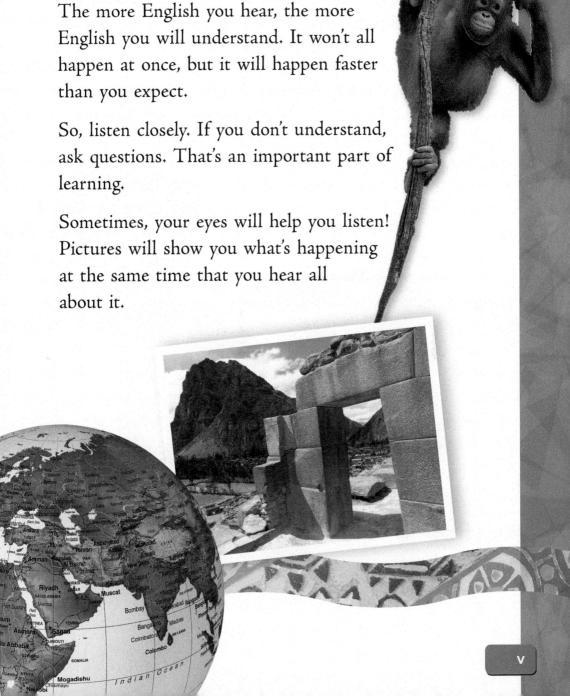

Listening

The more English you hear, the more English you will understand. It won't all happen at once, but it will happen faster than you expect.

So, listen closely. If you don't understand, ask questions. That's an important part of learning.

Sometimes, your eyes will help you listen! Pictures will show you what's happening at the same time that you hear all about it.

Speaking

With this program, you'll learn and say new English words every day. You'll use them, too. You'll learn how to put the words together. Your English will get better and better.

Speaking English will help you in almost every part of your life. You'll be able to share information and ideas. You'll be able to express your own thoughts and opinions in English.

Reading

Most of the words you will see in the United States are written in English. You can see words everywhere. They tell you the news. They give you the information you need. They tell you stories, and they tell you what people are like all around the world. Without words, you'd miss out on almost everything!

In this book, you will learn how to understand simple ideas that are written down. Then you'll start to understand written ideas that aren't so simple. Keep going, and you'll get there.

Writing

You'll listen to English, speak it, and read it, too. As you do, you'll learn more words and more ways to put them together. At the same time, you'll be using what you learn to write in English.

You'll learn about different kinds of writing. You'll write your own letters, stories, and reports in English. Your teacher will show you how to start each writing project. Then you'll learn how to improve your work and make it really great!

GET GOING

The most important piece of the puzzle is you. You'll know when you're doing well and when you need help. It will be your job to push yourself ahead.

Keep going. You're on your way to English.

Contents

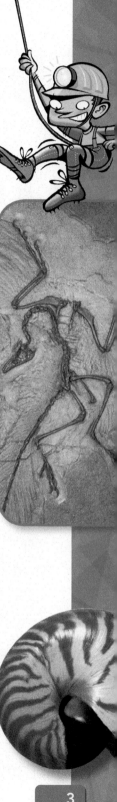

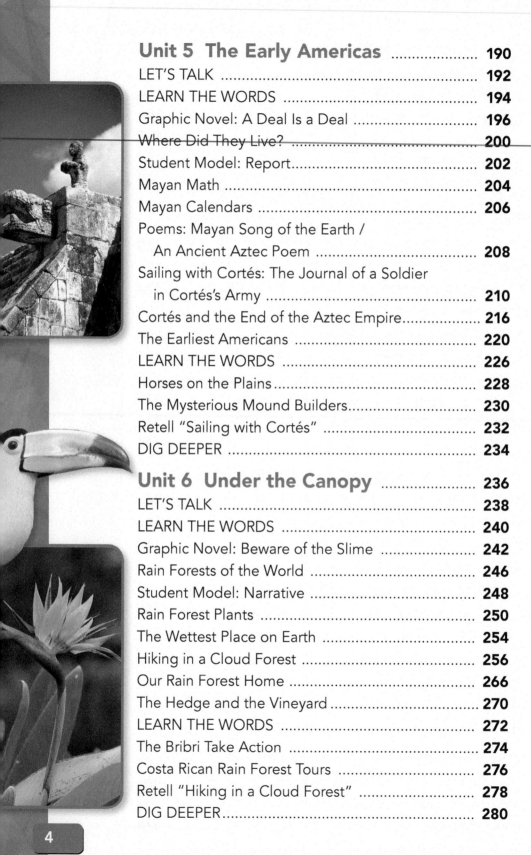

AMERICAN JOURNEYS

The **BIG** Question

What might it be like to start a new life in a new place?

☐ What might be difficult about moving to a new place?

☐ What things might be the same as they were in the old home?

☐ What things might be different in a new place?

Let's Talk

Why do people move to new places?

1. **What is your family's homeland?**

   My family's homeland is…

   ☐  ☐  ☐

   ☐  ☐

2. **Why do immigrants leave their homelands?**

   Immigrants move to seek…

   ☐ employment.

   ☐ better education.

   ☐ better treatment.

   ☐ freedom of religion.

3. What struggles do some immigrants have?

Some immigrants struggle with...

☐ a new place to settle.

☐ a new language.

☐ new traditions.

☐ new friends.

4. How do people move to a new place?

People move by...

☐ van.    ☐ jet.

☐ train.    ☐ ship.

☐ bus.

Say **more!**

homeland
immigrant
freedom
language
trade
treatment
religion
settle

Theme Vocabulary

 The easiest way to remember the meaning of a new word is to use the word. As you discuss coming to a new country, use these vocabulary words. Use them when you read and write about this topic, too.

Read the word.
Look at the picture.
Listen to your teacher.

homeland

immigrant

freedom

language

trade

treatment

religion

settle

Which Picture?

Look at the vocabulary cards. Choose one picture. Don't tell anyone what it is! Describe the picture. See if your partner can guess which picture you chose.

Dog Talk

Jamal   Victor   Alicia   Leo

1

2

What is in the box?

My dog, Leo.

3

Leo says hello.

Woof, woof!

4

Hey! You can't bring pets on the bus!

Leo is not my pet. I am his translator.

5

How can you be his translator?

I'm bilingual. I speak English and Dog.

No way.

Arf, arf!

6

"Arf, arf!" That's how you say "good morning" in Dog.

7

I'm trilingual. I speak English, Spanish, and Dog.

8

"Guau guau!" That's how you say "nice to meet you" in Dog.

9

"Guau guau!" is not how dogs talk.

That is how a dog talks in Peru.

10

 9 Formal/Informal Language "Nice to meet you" is a polite way to respond when you are introduced to someone. What would you say to a classmate you meet for the first time?

11) **Formal/Informal Language** Saying someone is "nuts" is another way to say the person is crazy. This idiom is only used in informal situations.

16 Why won't he settle down? He's having a fit.

17 I'll tell you why. Dogs don't have a language.

18 The only way to talk to a dog is through its stomach.

19

20 He says the sandwich is delicious!

 16 **Formal/Informal Language** "To have a fit" is an informal expression that means "to get very upset and angry."

Welcome to America

by Stan Pulaski

The United States welcomed 30 million **immigrants** to its shores between 1815 and 1915. These immigrants came from many places. Most came from countries in Europe.

Immigrants left their **homelands** to **seek** a better life. They were looking for **education**, **employment**, **freedom** of **religion**, and better **treatment**. Often they were running away from hard times. They wanted a chance to start a new life.

In those days, immigrants from Europe traveled by ship. They sailed to New York, Boston, and other ports on the East Coast. Immigrants from China, Japan, and the rest of Asia sailed to San Francisco and other West Coast ports. They hoped the difficult **voyage** would be worth the **struggle**.

The voyage to the United States was long and difficult.

Some immigrants stayed close to the port cities where they **arrived**. Others traveled inland. They went where there was a lot of land and few people. They went to farm, open a store, work on the railroad, or do other jobs.

In the 1800s, the United States had a lot of open land. Companies made ads to sell the land. People from American cities, not just immigrants, went to **settle** on it.

Immigrants often went to areas where other people from their homeland had already settled. It was easier for them to make a new start near other people who spoke the same **language** and shared the same religion and **traditions**.

THE
IMMIGRANTS' GUIDE
TO THE MOST
FERTILE LANDS
OF
KANSAS
The best part of the West in which

To buy a Grain Farm,
To buy a Stock Farm,
To buy a Sheep Ranch,
To open a Store, or
To practice a Profession.

Multitudes in the older States can improve their condition by selling out and emigrating to these fertile fields, which can be purchased at $2.50 to $6.00 an acre on eleven years credit.

Maps and General Information obtained FREE by sending your address to

S. J. GILMORE,
Land Commissioner, KANSAS CITY, MO.

Or to

R. B. GRIFFEN
Emigration Agent
Manchester, Iowa

Bikes—Yes!

by Jenny Wilson

Riding a bike is fun. It's also great exercise. When we are biking, we're also breathing fresh air, which is a good thing. We're working our muscles and building our strength. Biking burns calories. In addition, studies show that kids who bike to school perform better than kids who get there by car or bus. We don't use bikes nearly as much as we should.

When do people ride bikes? The answer is mostly after school, after work, on weekends, and on vacation. For most of the rest of the time, people use their gas-guzzling cars to get around. That's a problem. We should cut down on the gas we use because Earth's resources are limited. Using cars less means less air pollution and traffic.

Cars—No!

Why do people use bikes only for fun? Maybe it's just a habit, but it's a bad habit. Families should switch from cars to bikes whenever possible. They need to ask, "What's the rush?" If it takes five minutes to drive to the store and fifteen minutes to ride a bike, we are talking about a difference of only ten minutes. That's not a big deal.

Some people don't bike more often because they are afraid of the traffic. That is an issue, but if we could get bike lanes in our town, then that problem would be solved, too.

We should all make a commitment to use bikes for trips under two miles and save cars for longer trips. Then car traffic and pollution would be cut, money would be saved, and people would be in better shape!

Coming to America

by Carole Taylor

▲ Immigrants from Europe arrive at Ellis Island in New York City during the late 1800s.

The most famous place where immigrants arrived in the United States was Ellis Island, in New York City. From 1892 to 1954, 12 million people entered the United States through Ellis Island.

As the immigrants arrived, they were checked and cleared for entry into the United States. People who were very sick were not allowed in.

Over the years, waves of immigrants arrived from different places. Each group added something new and special to the American mix.

The United States fought a war in Vietnam that ended in the 1970s. After the war, many Vietnamese suffered bad treatment from their government. Thousands decided to leave their homeland for the United States. Some of the first to leave had to begin their trip in crowded and unsafe boats.

Once the Vietnamese immigrants arrived, they quickly settled into life in the United States. Now there are almost two million Vietnamese-Americans. Most live in California, Texas, Florida, Washington, and Virginia.

Many immigrants today come from Mexico. Like most immigrants, they come seeking jobs and **opportunities** so they can create a better life for their families.

Mexican-Americans bring their rich cultural traditions with them to the United States. They bring their language, religion, foods, and festivals. Just as they adapt to their new life in America, America also adapts as it welcomes in its new arrivals.

In the past, most immigrants came from Europe. Now immigrants come from more places in the world. Many come from Mexico, Asia, Africa, and Central and South America.

Many immigrants do well in the United States. They struggle to get ahead. They want to make sure their children have a better life than they had. They make sure their children get a good education. Education means more opportunities for employment.

 Immigrants from Mexico do all kinds of jobs. They work in business and in **trade**. They work in offices and in hospitals.

The United States has always been a country of immigrants. In fact, in recent years, the number of United States residents born outside the U.S. has been rising. In 2010, about one-tenth of U.S. residents were born in another country.

▲ This boy is the son of immigrants from India. He won the National Spelling Bee.

Prove It

What are two details that support the idea that Americans have come from many parts of the world?

Being Here

by Dina McClellan

Weather's colder, food's too bland,
I miss the ocean and the sand.
Days are shorter, words are new
And don't mean what you want them to.
Buildings taller, cars too wide.
Can't walk places. Have to ride.
Things cost more, but they're worth less.
I miss the old men playing chess.

Dogs are big, phones are small
(And I don't see their point at all).
Bedroom's cramped. It's hard to clean it.
People smile when they don't mean it.
Different colors, different clothes,
Different names for different shows.

It's hard to figure out what's what
When everything that *was*
    is *not*.

Too Many NEWS

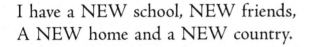

by Patricia J. Murphy

I have a NEW school, NEW friends,
A NEW home and a NEW country.

I speak a NEW language, try NEW foods,
Have NEW freedoms, try NEW customs,
And see NEW faces.

Right now they are like
A pair of shoes that is too big.

I hope that NEW things will soon feel OLD—
Like OLD friends, the OLD neighborhood,
My OLD country.

I want these new shoes
To fit me because I know
They will take me great places.

VOICES

by Nina Denkova

Boris slid into his chair at the breakfast table. His cousin Liliya was already eating pancakes. Grandmother was making lunches for everyone to take to work or to school. Aunt Stevka was talking on her cell phone. Mama was at the stove making more pancakes.

Just the smell of the oil sizzling in the pan could make Boris hungry. Mom made the best pancakes. They were as thin and light as lace. Today, though, Boris was too nervous to be hungry. He sipped at the milk he had poured for himself.

This would be his first day at his new school. His family had lived in the United States for six months, but they had just moved to San Francisco. Aunt Stevka, a nurse, already lived here. She had invited them to move in with her. Sharing housing would give all of them a better life. So Boris was starting over again for the second time this year.

The kitchen was full of voices—and languages! Mama chatted in Bulgarian with Grandmother. Aunt Stevka spoke in English on the phone. The television was tuned to the Russian channel. In the old days, everyone in Bulgaria learned both Bulgarian and Russian at school. So the adults in Boris's family spoke it well, though Boris and Liliya didn't. Mama and Grandmother enjoyed the Russian TV shows on cable.

"Learning English is what's important now," Aunt Stevka had told Boris. "I'll speak only English to you from now on."

"He has to remember who he is!" Grandmother would say. "I'm not speaking anything to him but Bulgarian."

Mama brought over a plate of pancakes for Boris. Aunt Stevka ended her phone call. One by one, the adults sat down to eat.

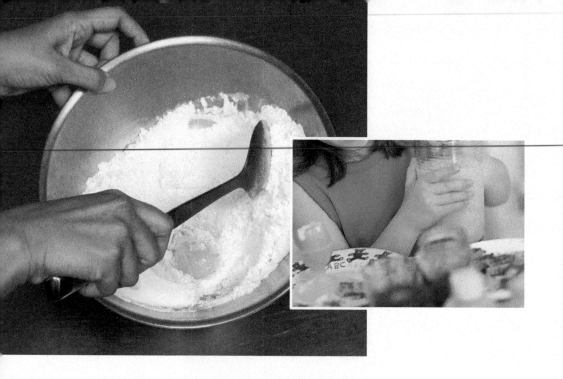

"Yum! I love it when you make pancakes," said Liliya in English. She had lived in the United States for most of her life. She hardly had an accent at all. Boris wondered if he would ever know as much English as Liliya did. She turned to Boris. "You're going to be in Ms. Rivera's class," she said in Bulgarian. "She's very nice. My friend's sister Mei is in her class."

"I just hope I get along with all the kids," said Boris.

"Just be quiet for the first few days until you can figure out who's who," advised Aunt Stevka. "Be polite to everyone."

"What—even to children who are rude to him? What are you teaching him?" said Grandmother. "Don't let anyone push you around," she said to Boris.

The others all joined in, even Lilya. Boris's head was starting to spin. Maybe he could just stay home and take classes online.

Somehow, he finished his breakfast. He gathered up his books and his lunch. All three adults hugged him before he left the house with Liliya. He could still hear them calling out advice halfway down the block.

At the school, Liliya ran to greet her girlfriends. Boris knew that it would not be cool to go into the school in a crowd of little girls. So he waited a moment and walked into the building alone.

He and Mama had already visited the principal's office the day before. So he knew his way there. Mr. Halloran greeted him. "Are you ready to meet your teacher and classmates?" the principal asked.

"Yes, sir," Boris said. It was not quite true, but he said it anyway.

Zoom In

What details show how everyone in the family tries to help Boris prepare for his new school?

Mr. Halloran led Boris up a staircase. Boris thought about what Mama would expect him to say. He knew how Grandmother would expect him to behave. He remembered Aunt Stevka's advice. Then he realized that they wouldn't be there in the classroom with him. Only his voice would be heard there. He could choose what to say and do next.

As Mr. Halloran brought him into the classroom, the bell rang. The class quieted down, and Ms. Rivera came forward. "Hello, Boris," she said, shaking Boris's hand.

"Class, today we have a new student," she said. "This is Boris. He's from Bulgaria. That is on the continent of Europe. Who can find Bulgaria on the map?"

Voices spoke up from all over the classroom. All of the words were in English. None of the children raised their hands, though. Maybe no one knew how to find Bulgaria on the map.

"Boris, show us where Bulgaria is," said Ms. Rivera.

Boris went over to the large map. He pointed to his home country. Even on the map, it looked far away from the United States.

"See, everyone? This is Bulgaria," said the teacher. Then she said something Boris did not expect. "Chris, your family came from Greece before you were born. That's right here next to Bulgaria. Farida, your family came from Egypt just two years ago. That's across the Mediterranean Sea from Bulgaria." She smiled at Boris. "My family came from the Philippines. Here it is on the map. It's in the Pacific Ocean. Somehow, we all found our way here to San Francisco."

Boris looked out at his class. He realized that he was not the only new person. He was just the only new person today. "Don't worry, Mama. Don't worry, Grandmother and Aunt Stevka," he thought. "This is going to work out well."

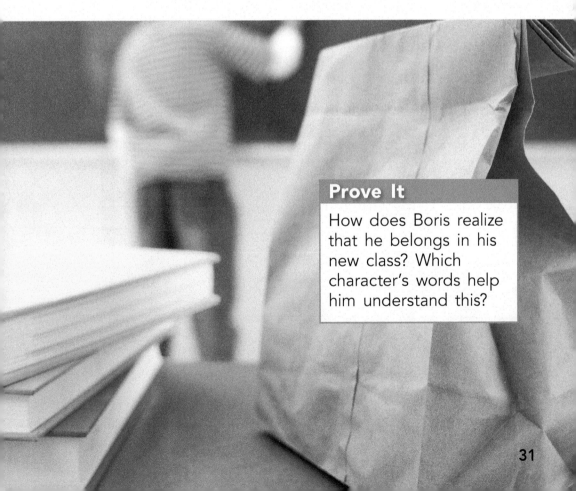

Prove It

How does Boris realize that he belongs in his new class? Which character's words help him understand this?

The New Girl

by Dina McClellan

Cast of Characters

KYLIE	LEELEE	RASHIDA
ANGELA	SO YUNG	OLDER WOMAN

Setting: The play takes place in a schoolyard in a big U.S. city. It is before the school bell. Kids are chatting, playing ball, shooting hoops. KYLIE, RASHIDA, SO YUNG, and LEELEE, classmates in the fourth grade, are in a corner by the fence, whispering.

KYLIE: *Psssst.* That's her.

SO YUNG: In the red sweater?

KYLIE: Her name is Angela. She's in my class.

SO YUNG: Where is she from?

KYLIE: She's from Trinidad.

SO YUNG: Where's Trinidad?

(No one answers.)

LEELEE: So what's she like?

KYLIE: She's nice.

RASHIDA: What else?

KYLIE (*shrugs*): She speaks English. That's what they speak in Trinidad.

RASHIDA: That's nice.

SO YUNG: She looks nice.

KYLIE: She *is* nice.

LEELEE: I think she's coming this way . . .

(ANGELA *walks over.*)

ANGELA (*smiling brightly*): Hi, Kylie.

KYLIE: Hey, Angela! How's everything going?

ANGELA (*still smiling*): Very well, thank you.

(*No one talks. They all stand around awkwardly.*)

KYLIE: Have you met my friends?

LEELEE: I'm Leelee. This is Rashida. And this is So Yung.

ANGELA: I love your hat, So Yung!

SO YUNG: Thanks, Angela.

ANGELA: And your boots, Leelee—they're so beautiful!

LEELEE: Thanks, Angela.

ANGELA: And I loved what you said in class today, Kylie—it was so smart!

SO YUNG: I don't believe it. Kylie said something *smart*?

(KYLIE *gives* SO YUNG *a playful shove.* SO YUNG *sticks out her tongue.*)

(*Just outside the fence, the* OLDER WOMAN *walks by with a small, bad-tempered dog. The dog barks and leaps toward the fence. Surprised,* ANGELA *backs up with a disgusted look.*)

KYLIE: Look at that cute dog. It looks just like my dog, Ritzy.

ANGELA (*looking worried*): Oh! What a . . . nice dog.

SO YUNG: You didn't look as if you liked that dog a second ago.

ANGELA (*even more anxious*): No, really, dogs are great. I didn't mean to hurt your feelings.

KYLIE: You don't have to like all dogs. In fact, you don't even have to like my dog. Why do you think you always have to like everything?

ANGELA (*hesitating at first*): My mother tells me, "Angela, be nice! Be nice so your new friends will like you."

LEELEE: That must get very tiring for you.

ANGELA (*almost whispering*): Sometimes.

KYLIE (*hugging ANGELA*): Oh, Angela! You don't have to be nice!

LEELEE: Well, you can be nice. (*Laughs.*) You just don't have to be PERFECTLY nice.

ANGELA (*sighing with relief*): Oh, I think I can do that.

Prove It

What details help you to know that this is a play?

35

from

Home of the Brave

by Katherine Applegate

People come to the United States for many reasons. Kek comes from an African country torn by war. He has lost most of his family. He is brought to this country to live with his aunt and his cousin, Ganwar. Dave is an American man whom Kek first calls "the helping man." Dave helps Kek get settled. Now all Kek has to do is fit in—somehow!

This story is told as a series of poems. As Kek's words show, things that are ordinary to most people can seem very strange to someone who had a different way of life.

Snow

When the flying boat
returns to earth at last,
I open my eyes
and gaze out the round window.
What is all the white? I whisper.
Where is all the world?

The helping man greets me
and there are many lines and questions
and pieces of paper.

At last I follow him outside.
We call that snow, he says.
Isn't it beautiful?
Do you like the cold?

I want to say
No, this cold is like claws on my skin!

I look around me.
Dead grass pokes through
the unkind blanket of white.
Everywhere the snow
sparkles with light
hard as high sun.
I close my eyes.
I try out my new English words:
How can you live
in this place called America?
It burns your eyes!
The man gives me a fat shirt

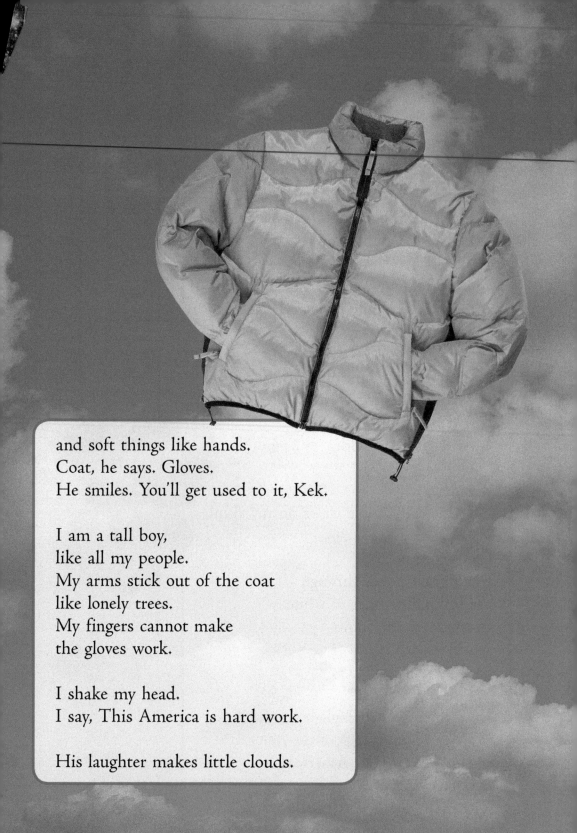

and soft things like hands.
Coat, he says. Gloves.
He smiles. You'll get used to it, Kek.

I am a tall boy,
like all my people.
My arms stick out of the coat
like lonely trees.
My fingers cannot make
the gloves work.

I shake my head.
I say, This America is hard work.

His laughter makes little clouds.

Dave drives Kek to an apartment. There, Kek sees his aunt and his cousin, Ganwar. He has not seen them in a long time. Kek will live with them. Everything that Dave teaches Kek makes him think of his homeland.

Lessons

I'll let you get settled, Dave says,
but first I'll give you some lessons.
Your aunt and your cousin know these things,
but you'll need to know them, too.

Number one, he says,
always lock your door.
Ganwar, show Kek what a key looks like.

In my old home,
my real home,
my father kept us safe.
We had no need for locks.

Number two, he says,
this is a light switch.
He pushes a tiny stick on the wall
and the room turns to night,
then blinks awake.

Zoom In

What are some of the things that make Kek feel that "This America is hard work"? What evidence can you use?

In my old home,
my real home,
the sun gave us light,
and the stars
watched us sleep.

This thermostat, Dave says,
helps keep you warm.
He pretends to shiver
to paint a picture for his words.

In my old home,
my real home,
we were a family,
and our laughter kept us warm.
We didn't need a magic switch
on a wall.

I nod to say yes,
I understand,
but I wonder if I will ever understand,
even if Dave stands here,
pointing and talking
forever.

Father

He had many cattle,
my father,
and the respect of our village,
but it was his voice that made him
a rich man among men.
His voice was deep,
like a storm coming,
but gentle,
like the rain ending.

My people are herders.
We move with the seasons,
with the wet and the dry,
so that the cattle
may be strong and well fed.
We cannot carry much with us,
and so our stories don't
make their homes
in heavy books.
We hold our stories
in our songs.

No one knew more songs
than my father,
and no one sang them
with a voice as clear and sure.

Prove It

What details from the story show how much Kek misses his father?

Learn the Words

arrive
education
employment
opportunity
seek
struggle
tradition
voyage

- Read the words on the list.
- Read the dialogue.
- Find the words.

*Immigrants had the **opportunity** to start a new life.*

*People left their homes to **seek** employment.*

1. Draw a Picture
Listening and Speaking

Your class is going to create a display for a museum. The display should show the reasons that people come to the United States. Draw a picture to show what you think is important. Share your picture with your partner. Talk about it.

2. You Are the Author
Writing

With a partner, think of words that describe how new immigrants might feel. Write the words. Use the words to write a poem about being in a new country. You can use the poems in this unit as a model. Share your poem with your partner.

3. New Traditions
Listening and Speaking

What new traditions do you think your family should celebrate? Think about something important that should be remembered. Create a holiday! Give your holiday a name. Tell about three traditions that should be included every year for your holiday.

4. Make a Chart
Graphic Organizer

Look at the chart. Why did people come to the United States in the past? Why do they come now? Complete the chart below using check marks (✓).

Why People Came	Back Then	Now
For opportunities		
For employment		
For freedom		

Food Facts

In the United States, eating is an adventure. There are so many different kinds of tasty foods. Many of these foods were brought to the United States by immigrants. Now, they are all part of American meals. Here are some fun food facts.

Mexico

Italy

China

Iran

India

Central America

Food	Origin	Fun Fact
Burrito	Mexico	*Burrito* means "little donkey" in Spanish.
Chocolate	Central America	Chocolate comes from cacao beans. These beans were once used as money.
Rice	China	Scientists have found pots of rice from 4000 B.C.
Curry	India	Curry is a blend of from 2 to 20 different spices.
Spinach	Iran	Spinach was once used as medicine.
Pizza	Italy	Pizza was first made for a king and a queen.

Albert Einstein: IMMIGRANT

by Alva O'Brien

One of the most famous immigrants to the United States was the scientist Albert Einstein. He was born in Germany in 1879. He moved to Italy to be with his parents and then to Switzerland. He studied to become a math and physics teacher. When he could not get a teaching job, he went to work in an office. In his spare time, he wrote scientific papers. One of them had his famous formula, "$e = mc^2$." Einstein won the Nobel Prize for Physics in 1921.

In 1933, while Einstein was visiting America, the Nazi party came to power in Germany. Einstein did not agree with what the Nazis were doing. He did not want to return to Germany. He stayed in the United States and got a position teaching at Princeton University. In 1940 he became an American citizen. He worked for peace until his death in 1955. His work as a scientist is still known all around the world.

Immigrants to America have always worked hard and made a big contribution. From actors to athletes, scientists to singers, in every field, the newcomers have made their mark.

FAMOUS Immigrants

NAME	FROM	CONTRIBUTION
Levi Strauss	Born in Germany in 1829. Died in 1902.	Invented denim blue jeans. His company still makes jeans today.
Frances Cabrini	Born in a part of Italy that was ruled by Austria, in 1850. Died in 1917.	Founded hospitals and homes for orphans all across the United States.
I.M. Pei	Born in China in 1917.	Architect. Designed the John Hancock Tower, the JFK Library, and the Rock and Roll Hall of Fame, among other buildings.
Gloria Estefan	Born in Cuba in 1957.	Pop singer and songwriter. She has sold over 100 million recordings worldwide.
Hakeem Olajuwon	Born in Nigeria in 1963.	NBA basketball player. From 1984 to 2002 he played center for the Houston Rockets and Toronto Raptors.

Retell "Voices"

"Voices" is a story about a boy going to a new school for the first time. Review the selection on pages 26–31. Look at the pictures on page 49.

- Beginning: Tell how Boris feels about school while he is still at home. Tell why he feels that way.

- Middle: Tell what happens as Boris goes into the school.

- End: Tell what happens in Boris's classroom. Tell how this makes him feel about school.

Use the pictures on page 49 to retell the story to your partner. As you retell each event, point to the correct picture. Use complete sentences.

Words you might use in your retelling:		
settle	arrive	immigrant
struggle	tradition	homeland

at home

into the school

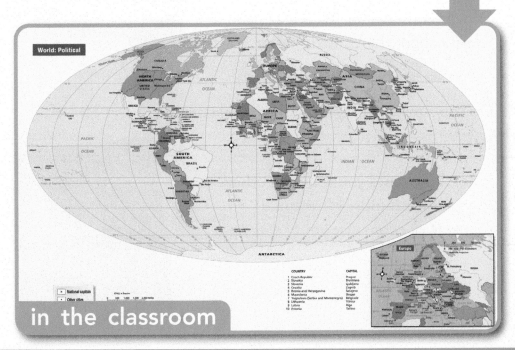

in the classroom

Dig Deeper

Look Back

Look at the selections "Voices," "The New Girl," and "Home of the Brave." Answer these questions on a sheet of paper.

1. Which selection is told by a character in the selection?

2. What words in that selection are clues that a character is telling his or her own story?

3. Which selection is a play? How do you know?

Talk About It

What details would you tell a friend or a relative about the United States?

What are the best things?

Do you agree or disagree with your classmates?

Why or why not?

If not, how could you convince others to change their minds? How could someone else convince you?

Conversation

 When you have a conversation, you talk. You also listen. You listen to the information your friend gives you. You listen to what your friend is asking you.

Talk to a partner. One of you will be person A.
The other will be person B.

Person A

Person B

Say hi.

Reply.
Ask your partner's name.

Reply.
Ask your partner's name.

Reply.
Ask your partner
a question.

Reply.
Ask your partner
a question.

Reply.
Say goodbye.

Across the
United States

The **BIG** Question

How does where we live affect how we live?

☐ How are the regions of the United States different?

☐ What are some places that people like to visit in the United States?

☐ What is the weather like in different parts of the United States?

1. **What are some landforms found in the United States?**

   The United States has…

   ☐ deserts.   ☐ valleys.

   ☐ plains.   ☐ lakes.

   ☐ hills.   ☐ mountains.

2. **What is your region like?**

   My region has…

   ☐ some lakes.

   ☐ low hills.

   ☐ flat land.

   ☐ ice all over.

3. Pretend you are a tourist.
   What do you want to see?

I want to see…

☐ the Grand Canyon.

☐ the ocean.

☐ some high peaks.

4. What can a region's climate be like?

A region can be…

☐ warm all year round.

☐ dry.

☐ rainy.

☐ cold in the winter.

Say **more!**

Learn the Words

geography
region
feature
valley
landform
coast
island
plain

The easiest way to remember the meaning of a new word is to use the word. As you discuss America's regions, use these vocabulary words. Use them when you read and write about the regions, too.

Read the word.
Look at the picture.
Listen to your teacher.

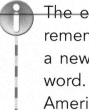

geography

region

feature

valley

landform

coast

island

plain

How Do You Feel?

Look at the vocabulary cards. Choose one picture
and tell how it makes you feel.

No Talking

Mrs. Baker | Tavon | Jake | Lilly | Nancy

The man in this picture was a great civil rights leader.

Does anybody know his name?

BROWN

Martin Luther King!

Actually, it's Martin Luther King *Junior*.

Very good, Jake.

 9) Formal/Informal Language A more informal way to say "No, I wasn't!" is, "No way!"

59

 12) **Formal/Informal Language** When Tavon thinks, "This stinks," he is expressing displeasure. Why do you think he thinks this instead of saying it out loud?

17) **Expressions** "I've had about enough of this" is an expression that means "I won't allow this behavior any longer."

61

A COUNTRY OF REGIONS

PACIFIC

OCEAN

UNITED

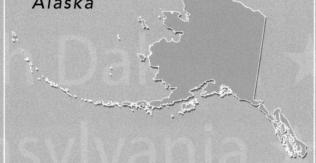

Alaska

Hawaii

The United States of America reaches from the Atlantic Ocean to the Pacific Ocean. That's more than 3,000 miles! There are 50 states in all. The states are in five **regions**.

STATES

N
W   E
S

ATLANTIC OCEAN

Gulf of Mexico

KEY
■ Northeast
■ Southeast
■ Midwest
☐ Southwest
■ West

Akimi Learns English

by Akimi Mogi

When I first moved to Los Angeles from Tokyo, I didn't know a word of English. My parents and older sister didn't, either.

We moved here for my sister. She was a famous violinist in Japan. She wanted to study music in America. I knew nothing about music. I just wanted to be an American kid, and I wanted to speak English. After a few weeks, I got to be friends with a boy in my class. He was always trying to talk to me. His name was Freddie. At first, my only English word was, "Hi!" So I said it a lot. "Hi! Hi! Hi!"

One day, I was in the school yard. Freddie came toward me holding half a sandwich. I said, "Hi!" And he handed me his sandwich.

Another day, Freddie invited me to see his new tree house. I went to the back yard. "Hi!" I said. Freddie helped me climb up the ladder. I don't know why. I never said I wanted to climb up the ladder.

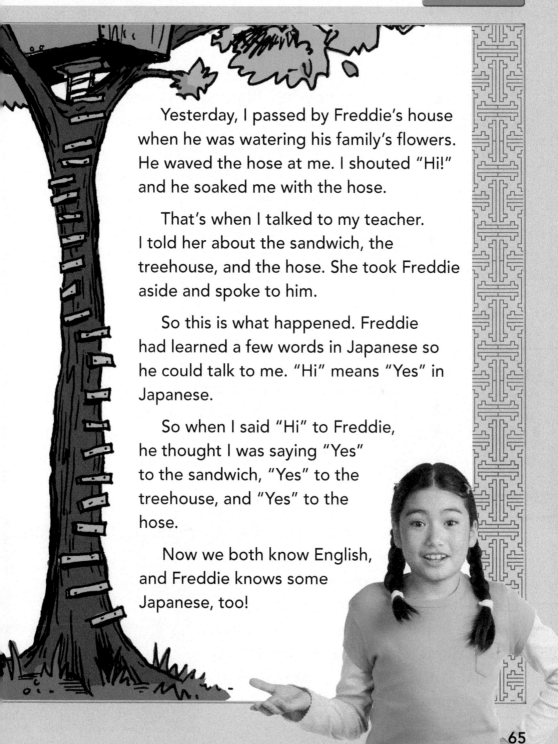

Yesterday, I passed by Freddie's house when he was watering his family's flowers. He waved the hose at me. I shouted "Hi!" and he soaked me with the hose.

That's when I talked to my teacher. I told her about the sandwich, the treehouse, and the hose. She took Freddie aside and spoke to him.

So this is what happened. Freddie had learned a few words in Japanese so he could talk to me. "Hi" means "Yes" in Japanese.

So when I said "Hi" to Freddie, he thought I was saying "Yes" to the sandwich, "Yes" to the treehouse, and "Yes" to the hose.

Now we both know English, and Freddie knows some Japanese, too!

Landforms

by Basil Green

If you travel across the United States, you can study its **geography**. Our country has almost every type of **landform**, from **plains** and deserts to mountains.

Here are some common landforms that you might see. Notice how they are the same and different. Some are wet, but others are dry. Some are flat, but others are bumpy and uneven. Some get a lot of rain. Others are dry.

desert

A desert is an area that gets little rain. Deserts are dry and can get very hot. They can be made of rocks, mountains, and sand. There are deserts in the West and Southwest regions of the United States.

swamp

A swamp is nothing at all like a desert. A swamp is always wet. It is a low-lying area where water collects. Certain trees like to grow in swamps. You can find swamps in many regions of the United States. Some of the biggest are in Florida. But watch out! Swamps can have alligators or crocodiles.

mountain

A mountain is land that rises high up. Mountains have rocky sides and peaks. They may be covered with snow, even in summer. A mountain range is a connected group or line of mountains.

plain

In contrast, a plain is a large, flat area of land. Plains are often covered with grass. They have few trees. Because they are so flat and have rich soil, plains are good places for growing crops and grazing cattle.

canyon

valley

Two landforms that are similar in some ways are **valleys** and canyons. A valley is a low area of land between two hills or mountains. Its sides slope gently in a wide curve. A canyon is like a valley between tall cliffs of rock. It has steep sides. A river often flows through the bottom of a valley or a canyon. Although valleys make good farmland, canyons usually do not.

river

Unlike mountains, valleys, deserts, or plains, some landforms are bodies of water. For example, a river is a large stream of fresh water. A river starts on higher ground. It flows into a lake or an ocean. Unless it is frozen or dry, a river is always moving. Some move quickly, with foaming whitewater, or waterfalls. Others move more slowly.

lake

A lake is usually a large body of fresh water with land all around it. Water flows into a lake from rivers or springs. Lake Superior is the biggest lake in the United States.

ocean

The largest bodies of water are oceans. Although oceans cover most of Earth, there are just five oceans: the Atlantic, the Pacific, the Indian, the Arctic, and the Southern oceans. The Pacific Ocean is the largest in the world. Unlike rivers and most lakes, oceans have salt water.

Different landforms and **features** lend themselves to different **land uses**. For example, you can grow more crops in a valley than on a steep mountain.

coast

A **coast** is land next to the sea or ocean. A coast can have cliffs or beaches. The coast is popular with **tourists**. However, the coast isn't just for surfing and playing in the sand. It also has **industry**. The fishing and shipping industries are based on the coasts.

island

An **island** is land with water all around it. An island can be found in an ocean, lake, or river. Islands are popular with tourists.

Prove It

What are some details that show how oceans are different from rivers?

Come See the WEST!

The West is a great place for a vacation. There is so much to see and do! Here are some **sights** that you can visit in five western states. Remember, Alaska and Hawaii are in special places. They are separate from the other 48 states. Alaska is in the far north. It is on the west coast, but high up, above Canada. Hawaii is far out in the Pacific Ocean. The state is made up of a group of tropical islands.

Alaska
Washington
Hawaii
Oregon
California

Alaska

+ **Glacier Bay National Park** Explore the rugged coastline by kayak.
+ **Denali National Park and Reserve** Denali is home to Mt. McKinley, the highest peak in North America.

Hawaii

+ **Volcanoes National Park** Visit this park to see two active volcanoes.
+ **Waikiki Beach** This is one of the best beaches for surfing.

Washington

+ **Seattle** See the entire city from the top of the Space Needle.
+ **Olympic National Park** Hike through meadows covered with wildflowers.

Oregon

+ **Portland Japanese Garden** It has paths and fish ponds.
+ **Oregon Coast Aquarium** One exhibit has a tunnel. Walking through it is like being underwater with the fish.

California

+ **San Francisco** The Golden Gate Bridge is one of the longest suspension bridges in the U.S.
+ **Redwoods National Park** The tallest trees on Earth grow here.

Snapshots of the United States

Do you know about the geography of five regions of the United States?

Look at the pictures. Read the captions and the rest of the text. See if you can figure out which regions are on the pages.

Which region is this?

People catch lobsters in the coastal waters.

Farmers **harvest** apples, corn, and pumpkins.

This is the smallest region of the United States. It has lots of people packed into a small space. This region has hills and valleys and a long stretch of coast. It is home to both the White Mountains and the Green Mountains. The region has several big cities, including the U.S. city with the most people. This city is New York City. Tourists like to visit New York to see sights such as the Empire State Building.

Zoom In

What extra information do the captions on this page give?

Now do you know which region this is? It's the Northeast!

73

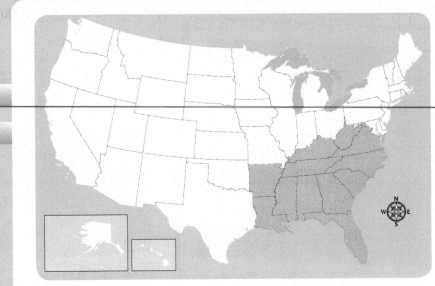

Which region is this?

Everglades National Park is the third-largest park in the lower 48 states. It is the largest wilderness east of the Mississippi River. It is home to many unusual plants and animals, including the American crocodile, the West Indian manatee, and the Florida panther. About one million people visit the park every year.

Atlanta, Georgia, has one of the largest and busiest airports in the country.

West Virginia **produces** more coal than most other states.

This region has the Atlantic Ocean to its east, the Gulf of Mexico to the south. It has many cities, such as Jacksonville, Florida; Charlotte, North Carolina; Memphis and Nashville, Tennessee; and New Orleans, Louisiana. There is a lot of **agriculture** in this region. Farmers harvest cotton, rice, sugar cane, oranges, and tomatoes. Some of the fun national parks you might want to visit in the region are Great Smoky Mountains National Park, Hot Springs National Park, and Mammoth Caves National Park.

Now do you know which region this is? It's the Southeast!

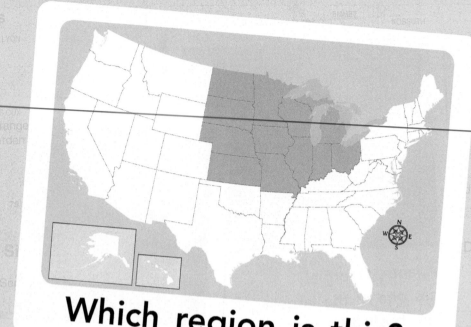

Which region is this?

Making cars is an important industry in Michigan. Cars are also produced in other states in the region, including Ohio, Indiana, Illinois, and Kentucky.

People use Lake Michigan for work and fun.

The faces of four U.S. Presidents are carved on Mount Rushmore.

This region is sometimes called the "heartland." That's because it is in the center of the United States. Its location makes it a central crossroads for the trucking industry, railroads, riverboats, and even air travel. The region has both heavy industry and agriculture. On flat plains, farmers harvest corn, soybeans, and wheat and raise cattle. The three biggest cities in the region are Chicago, Indianapolis, and Columbus. It also has beautiful natural areas. In the Badlands National Park, you can find old fossils. In the Boundary Waters, you can canoe in the area between the United States and Canada.

Zoom In

What information do you get from the map on page 76?

Now do you know which region this is?   It's the Midwest!

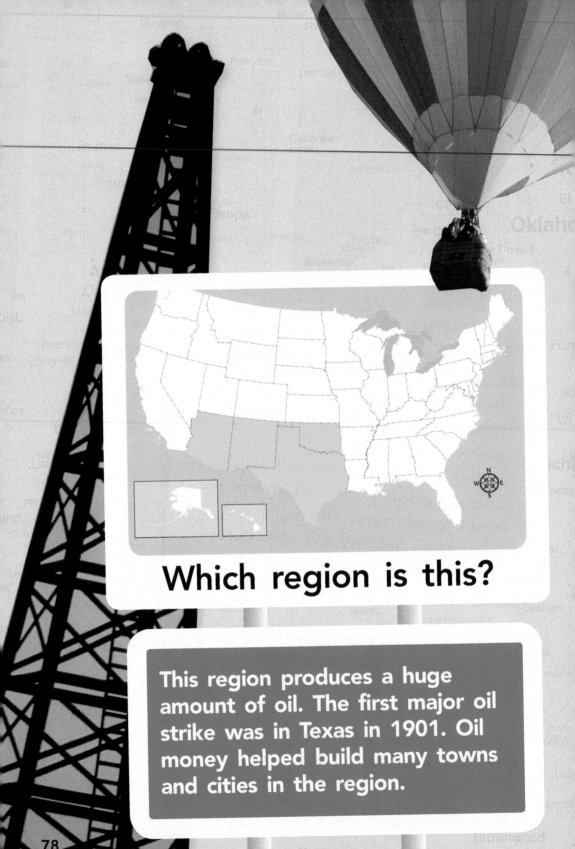

Which region is this?

This region produces a huge amount of oil. The first major oil strike was in Texas in 1901. Oil money helped build many towns and cities in the region.

Much of this region is very dry. Cactus and sagebrush grow in the deserts. A good land use for the wide open spaces is grazing cattle. The region also has a lot of wildlife, including bighorn sheep, bobcats, coyotes, and mountain lions. It has many interesting features in the landscape. That's why it has so many popular national parks. In addition to the Grand Canyon, there are Arches, Bryce Canyon, and Zion National Parks; Navajo, Four Corners, and White Sands National Monuments; plus Monument Valley and many others. Lots of people move here when they retire.

The Grand Canyon has visitors from all over the world.

Houston, Texas, is the fourth-largest city in the United States.

Now do you know which region this is?   It's the Southwest!

US ROUTE 101

Which region is this?

This region is a great place for sports of all kinds. People ski and snowboard in the Rocky Mountains. They surf and swim off the coasts of California and Hawaii. Kayaking and canoeing are popular on the region's rivers and lakes.

Many homes are made from trees from Washington State.

Alaska is partly covered in ice. Fewer plants grow here than in most other states.

This is a region of contrasts. It has bustling cities and natural wonders, tall mountains and low valleys. Death Valley in California is the lowest, driest, and hottest spot in the United States. Alaska has the country's tallest mountains. Some famous cities in the region include Las Vegas, Los Angeles, San Francisco, Salt Lake City, and Denver. Hollywood is the center of the movie industry. This region has some of the most beautiful national parks, including Glacier, Yosemite, and Yellowstone. In 1959, Alaska and Hawaii were the 49th and 50th states to join the United States.

Prove It

Where on this page do you find the answer to the question on page 80?

Now do you know which region this is?   It's the West!

How Water Came to Dry Lands

A Navajo Folktale
retold by Nomi J. Waldman

Navajos call themselves *Díne*, which means "the people." They live in the American southwest.

NAVAJO NATION

Utah

Colorado

Arizona

New Mexico

This Navajo folktale tells the story of how Snail and Deer Man brought water to the land. Because they live in a dry area, water is especially important to the Navajo people.

* * *

Long ago, Deer Man and Blue Bird Woman led the people to this world. They found a land of mesas and bright sunlight. It had no running waters—no streams, no brooks, no creeks. There was only a wide, muddy lake with water that was not fit to drink.

83

The people complained so much that their voices filled Blue Bird Woman's ears. She told her husband, "We cannot live here without fresh water."

Deer Man agreed. "If I had a few drops of fresh water, I could sing the water chant," he said. "I could turn the drops into a running river." There was only one thing to do.

Deer Man gathered the people together.

"We must have water," he said. "There is a spring that flows beneath the ocean. Can someone bring back a bottle of fresh water?"

He waited.

Then a very soft voice said, "I will."

It was none other than tiny Snail.

Snail was small and slow, but Deer Man welcomed her help. He tied the water bottle onto Snail's back.

The people watched as Snail went slowly to the ocean. Some shook their heads and said, "She's so small, and the bottle is so big!"

Deer Man knew the bottle was in safe hands.

Zoom In

What problem do the people have at the beginning of this folktale?

When Snail finally returned, everyone was asleep. Slowly, the exhausted Snail climbed the hill to her home. She was so tired that she dragged the water bottle on the ground. She did not see that a hole formed in the bottle. All the water was running out of it!

In the morning, Deer Man saw the water running down the hill. He began to sing the water chant. He sang, and the water sang, too. It turned into a wide river that ran to the ocean.

He said, "Now, thanks to Snail, we will always have fresh water."

Prove It

How is the Navajo people's real life reflected in the plot of this folktale? What evidence did you use?

The Great Colorado River runs to the ocean. Smaller rivers, like the one in this story, run to the Colorado.

Learn the Words

land use
agriculture
harvest
industry
produce
sight
tourist

- Read the words on the list.
- Read the dialogue.
- Find the words.

There has always been **agriculture** in this region.

Now there is **industry** here, too.

Land use depends a lot on rainfall.

You can't **produce** great crops in a desert!

1. You Are the Reporter
Writing

Pretend you are a reporter. You will talk to someone in the picture. What would you ask that person about the job they do? Write down five questions. Share those questions with your partner. Talk about ways to make the questions better.

2. Make a Chart
Graphic Organizer

Ask 5 classmates whether they have ever been to a farm. Tally their responses. Share your findings with your partner.

Have you ever been to a farm?	
Yes	No

3. Make a Drawing
Listening and Speaking

What tourist sight should be built in your community? Should it be a building? A bridge? Something else? Draw a picture showing your idea. Show the picture to your partner. Answer any questions your partner asks about the picture.

4. Write a Postcard
Writing

Did you ever see an interesting tourist sight? How did it make you feel? Write a postcard to a friend. Look at the selection "Snapshots of the United States" for ideas. Tell about the sight. Tell how you felt seeing it. Share your postcard with your class.

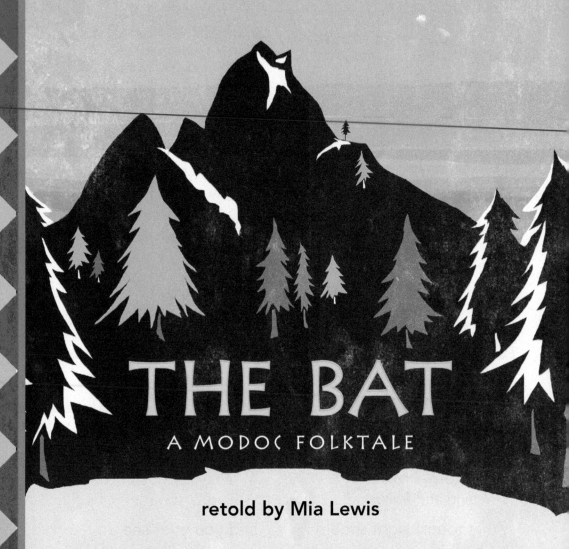

THE BAT

A MODOC FOLKTALE

retold by Mia Lewis

The Modoc are a Native American people originally from the eastern border region between California and Oregon. The Modoc lived in the area for thousand of years. They gathered food from the forest, hunted, and fished. They lived according to the seasons. They told stories explaining the natural world.

Here is a Modoc tale about a bat. Is Bat a bird or a beast? Bat tries to play it both ways, but he ends up on his own.

Once, long ago, there was a battle between the birds and the beasts. Everything that flew joined together to fight everything that walked. It was terrible.

Bat wasn't sure where he belonged. Should he fight with the birds in the air or the beasts on the ground? He decided to join the birds.

As luck would have it, on that first day of fighting, the beasts beat the birds. As soon as bat saw that his side was going to lose, he slipped away. He hid under a log and waited until the battle was over. When the beasts came walking by, he came out from under the log and joined them.

"Hey!" said one of the animals. "Weren't you just fighting on the birds' side? Go away! We don't want you here with us."

"Oh no," said Bat, "I am not a bird! Have you ever seen a bird with teeth or fur? Of course not! I am one of you."

The animals did not like it much, but they let Bat stay with them.

On the next day, the battle started over again. Bat was fighting on the ground with the beasts. But this time, the birds had the upper hand. They beat the beasts easily.

Bat saw soon enough that the beasts were getting beaten. Once again he slipped away and hid under a log. When the birds flew past, he flew out and joined them. It didn't take long for one of the birds to notice Bat.

"Go away, Bat!" said one of the birds. "You do not belong here with us. We saw you fighting on the beasts' side. You are our enemy!"

"Please," replied Bat. "Don't be foolish. Can't you see I have wings? Have you ever heard of a beast who could fly through the air? I didn't think so! I am one of you."

The birds did not like it, but they let Bat stay with them.

The war went on and on. Every day Bat crept away to join whichever side had won the battle that day. He went back and forth, back and forth, until finally the war was over.

At the end of the war, the birds and the beasts got together. They wanted to decide what to do with Bat. Where did he belong, with the birds or with the beasts? Neither group liked how he had behaved during the war.

"Bat," they said, "from this day on, you will not have any friends—neither the birds who fly in the air, nor the beasts who walk on the ground. For the rest of your days you will fly only at night, all alone."

Bat slipped away to hide in a cave until it was night. If you wait until the sun sets, you might see him flying.

Prove It

What proof does Bat use to say that he is a beast and not a bird?

Retell "Snapshots of the United States"

> When you retell a selection, you give only the important ideas and details. Using words such as *for example*, *is like*, and *including* will help readers understand your retelling.

"Snapshots of the United States" tells about regions of the United States. Review the selection on pages 72–81. Look at the map and pictures on page 95.

■ The Northeast: Give two important details about the Northeast.

■ The Southeast and the Midwest: Give two important details about each region.

■ The Southwest and the West: Give two important details about each region.

Use the map and the pictures on page 95 to retell the selection to your partner. As you give each important detail, point to the correct region. Use complete sentences.

Words you might use in your retelling:		
region	geography	coast
plain	tourist	produce

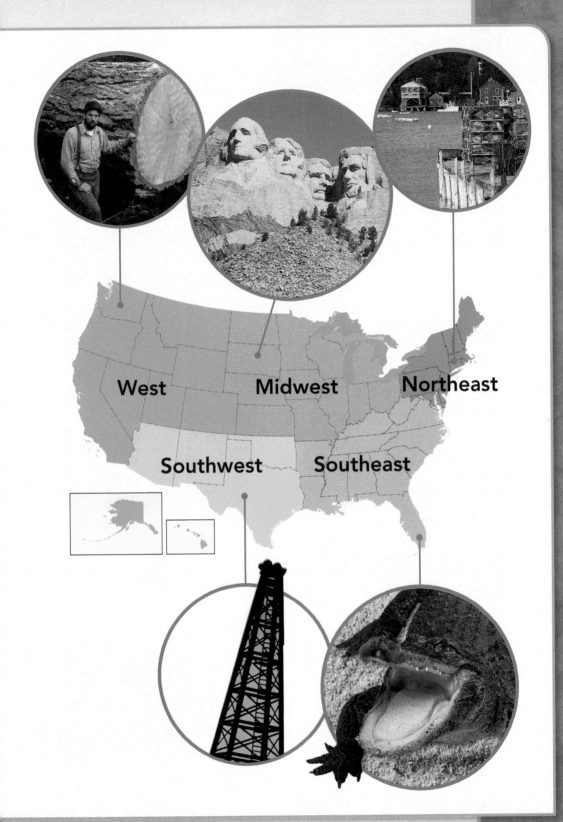

West

Midwest

Northeast

Southwest

Southeast

Dig Deeper

Look Back

Find the selection that tells mainly about landforms of the United States. Answer these questions on a sheet of paper.

1. What is the title of the selection?

2. What landform does the writer say is like a canyon?

3. What landform does the writer say is very different from a desert?

4. What landform has water all around it?

Talk About It

Here are some words that can describe Alaska.

Alaska is icy.

Alaska is icy and hilly.

Alaska is icy and hilly and snowy.

Alaska is icy and hilly and snowy and beautiful.

Think of another place. It could be a place from this unit. Work with a partner to describe it. Add more words.

Conversation

 Sometimes you have to ask for something. Maybe you need help. Maybe you need permission to do something. There is a polite way to ask for things. Use the word please when you ask. Say thank you when someone answers you or helps you.

Talk to a partner. One of you will be person A. The other will be person B.

Person A

Person B

Ask permission to do something.

Reply. Ask a question.

Reply. Ask to borrow something.

Reply.

Thank your partner.

Reply. (What do you say when someone thanks you?)

OUR CHANGING EARTH

The **BIG** Question

How does Earth change?

☐ What adventures can people have when they explore Earth?

☐ What do scientists learn when they study how Earth changes?

☐ How much do you think Earth has changed since you were born?

What forces change Earth's landforms?

1. **What can ice do?**

   Ice can...

   ☐ form a glacier.

   ☐ melt.

   ☐ crack stone.

   ☐ break with a loud sound.

2. **How can water change the land?**

   Water can...

   ☐ freeze into ice.

   ☐ flood the land.

   ☐ cause erosion.

   ☐ wear down rock.

3. What can a cave system have in it?

A cave system can have…

☐ limestone.

☐ darkness.

☐ lakes and rivers.

☐ tunnels.

4. How quickly does land change?

Land can change…

☐ overnight, from a flood or an earthquake.

☐ over several years, when people build on it.

☐ over millions of years, from the weather.

Say **more!**

101

Learn the Words

geology

weathering

erosion

deposition

force

glacier

cliff

break down

Theme Vocabulary

The easiest way to remember the meaning of a new word is to use the word. As you discuss the changing Earth, use these vocabulary words. Use them when you read and write about the changing Earth, too.

Read the word.
Look at the picture.
Listen to your teacher.

geology

weathering

erosion

deposition

force

glacier

cliff

break down

Match the Pictures

Look at the vocabulary cards. Choose two pictures that go
together. Tell why you think they go together.

Rasheed   Tim

5 **Formal/Informal Language** "Knock it off" is another way to say "stop it." Is this expression formal language or informal language?

 9 **Formal/Informal Language** "Hit the road" is an informal expression. What do you think it means?

Because I ate it!!!

I *ate* it because I *hate* it!

You know what? I hate it, too.

Give my hat a shot.

Now that's more like it!

 18 **Formal/Informal Language** When you "give something a shot," you try it. How could you say "Give my hat a shot" in a more formal way?

107

The Glaciers of Mount Hood

by Mia Lewis

Mount Hood is a mountain in the north of Oregon. It is part of the Cascades Mountain chain. It is not far from the city of Portland. Mount Hood is popular for hiking and climbing.

Mount Hood wears a beautiful cap of snow. Under the snow are 12 **glaciers**. The biggest is Eliot Glacier.

How did twelve glaciers get to the top of Mount Hood? Thousands of years ago, this land was much colder. The Cascade Mountains were covered with a thick **layer** of ice. When the climate got warmer, most of that ice melted. The Mount Hood glaciers are the ice that stayed.

A glacier is made of snow and ice that stays year round. It moves very slowly. It is like a frozen river creeping down a hill. A glacier gets big cracks in it as it moves. Glaciers are very heavy. They crush and scratch the rock below. They shape the earth as they move.

A glacier can collect rocks and soil as it melts and freezes. As it travels downhill, it deposits the rocks and dirt in new places. By this **process**, the glacier **alters** the shape of the land.

A glacier gets bigger during cold periods and smaller in warm periods. For the last 100 years, glaciers all over the world have been melting and shrinking.

Eliot Glacier stretches from the top all the way down the north side of the mountain. It is almost 300 feet thick in places. Sometimes it moves as much as 22 feet in one year! The water melting off the glacier becomes Eliot Creek. This creek waters the fruit orchards farther down the mountain.

> ## Prove It
> What details show that glaciers can change the land?

Poem

Things I Cannot Count

by Ross Radzykewycz

The number of grains of sand on a beach

The number of branches too high to reach

The number of snowflakes falling down

The number of rocks coming out of the ground

The number of mountaintops too steep to climb

The number of caves as ancient as time

The number of ants and spiders and fleas

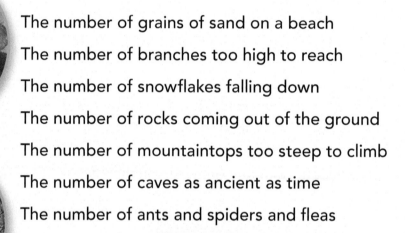

The number of puffs in a summertime breeze

The number of birds that fly through the air

The number of points from Here to There

The number of fossils etched in stone

The number of secrets not yet known

The number of drops there are in the sea

The number that reaches Infinity

Earth Science Storyteller

by Katie Sharp

Christa Sadler tells a story of Earth. She is a guide in the Grand **Canyon**. She takes people down the Colorado River by raft.

Christa's rafts are people-powered. That means that Christa and the other people in the raft all paddle to keep the raft going. Christa thinks this is more fun than letting a motor do all the work.

Christa fell in love with the Colorado River when she was in college. That's when she first saw it. Right away, Christa knew she was going to live, work, and play on the river.

To Christa, every river trip is different. She loves the excitement of paddling down the river. She loves the stillness of the nights spent outdoors in a tent. She loves teaching visitors about the Grand Canyon.

Christa didn't just show up and become a river guide. She had to learn how. She took a training course. In that course, she learned about all the gear she would use. She learned different kinds of paddle strokes for different parts of the river. In some places, the river rushes around rocks and gets pretty wild. River guides need to know how to keep the raft and its riders safe.

Today, Christa takes tourists on trips. She sets up the camp, and she even cooks the meals! Of course, she also tells the tourists about the canyon. She points out animals, birds, and different kinds of rocks.

For Christa, the canyon is like a book that is thousands of years old. The layers of the canyon are the book's chapters. Each layer shows how the river wore through the land, little by little.

Christa makes sure her passengers have a safe, exciting ride.

My Trip Through the Grand Canyon

by Eva Anderson

Last summer I went on a rafting trip on the Colorado River, through the Grand Canyon. It was the trip of a lifetime! My family was lucky to have Christa Sadler as our river guide. Christa was amazing. She knows everything about the river. She knows about the **geology** of the canyon, the birds and animals, the best places to camp, and the best hikes. Best of all, she loves to share what she knows.

Planning started long before we hit the water. We packed carefully because there is not much room in the boat. Christa and her company arranged for most of the gear we needed. We had tents, sleeping bags, life jackets, dry bags, and food.

The trip started at Lee's Ferry. After a safety talk, Christa made sure our inflatable paddleboat was loaded up. My parents and I, my cousin Matt, and a couple from Canada all got in the raft. Christa sat at the back. The rest of us helped to paddle! I was glad we weren't in a noisy motorboat.

As soon as we got on the water, things got interesting. In the Upper Canyon the river twists and turns. There is so much to look at! Christa told us about the layers in the rock **cliffs** and the geology of the area.

When we got to our first campsite, we pitched our tents. Christa cooked a delicious meal. We sat around the fire and told stories. I couldn't believe the stars! Christa told us many of their names. Every night we learned more.

In the Lower Canyon, there are a lot of rapids. The biggest of all is Lava Falls. It was so scary and exciting, but I felt safe with Christa guiding us. The river water is very cold, but the sun is hot so you dry out quickly. Luckily our gear was safely stored in the dry bags.

When the trip was over I felt ten feet tall. The trip changed everything for me. Now I know I want to spend my life working outdoors.

Prove It

What details show that the rafting trip was educational as well as being fun and exciting?

Stronger Than Rock

by Judy Bailey

"Wow!" I said, looking over the rim of the Grand Canyon.

"Yup. It's a long way down!" said Max.

Our class was about to hike to the bottom of the canyon. The view from the top was unbelievable. I had seen photographs, but in real life it was so much more amazing.

"The Grand Canyon is 277 miles long," said our guide, Elena. "It's 1 mile deep, and it's between 1 and 18 miles wide."

"What will we see at the bottom?" I asked.

"You'll see what has made the Grand Canyon so grand," said Elena.

The canyon was a giant gash in the land. Its steep walls were made of layers of colored rocks. We could see red, yellow, tan, and green.

"It's like a stack of colorful pancakes," said Max. Max is always hungry, so everything reminds him of food.

Zoom In

Which character is telling the story? How do you know?

I tried to think how anything could have carved such a deep canyon. "What's stronger than rock?" I wondered out loud.

"Many things can be stronger than rock," said Elena.

Our group walked down the path. "We're not just going down," said Elena. "In a way, we're also going back in time. The rocks at the bottom are older than the ones at the top."

"Hey, Trong," Max called out to me, "we're in a time machine."

"Kcit, kcit, kcit..." I said, laughing. "Get it? That's 'Tick, tick, tick' backwards."

"Very clever," groaned Max.

Just then, a bird flew off the canyon wall. Small rocks tumbled down the steep cliff.

"Wow!" I said. "That bird made those rocks fall."

"Is that what formed the canyon?" asked Max. "Birds' feet throwing rocks around?"

Elena said, "Something small *can* alter the land. Even little rockslides can **break down** a rock wall."

An hour later, the group stopped to rest. A gust of wind blew dust into the air.

"There's another clue," said Elena. "Wind wears down rock. Also, extreme heat and cold can break rock apart."

"Now we have a whole list of things stronger than rock!" said Max.

Finally the class reached the canyon floor. There, we saw a fast-moving river.

"That's it!" I said. "The river helped make the canyon. It wore through the rock."

"Well done," said Elena. "The Colorado River is the main 'digger' of the Grand Canyon."

"So, water, wind, heat, and cold are all stronger than stone, right?" I asked.

"Don't forget rock-throwing birds!" laughed Max.

"There's one other thing to remember," said Elena. "All these forces worked over millions of years. So, time is also stronger than rock."

"Speaking of time," said Max, "I think it must be time for lunch. Dig in, everyone!"

Prove It

What does the group decide is the main "digger" of the Grand Canyon? What details in the story tell that?

That's a Long River!

The Colorado River flows through the Grand Canyon. It's 1,450 miles long.

The First Discovery

from *Journey to the Bottomless Pit*
by Elizabeth Mitchell

In 1838, Stephen Bishop is an enslaved African American. He is a tour guide in Mammoth Cave, Kentucky, for his boss, Archibald Miller. Bishop leads visitors through the tunnels. The only light down there comes from candles. Some parts of the cave have names like Steamboat Rock and the Bottomless Pit.

One day, Stephen plans a trip alone. He wants to explore parts of the cave that no one knows about. He asks Nita, the cook, to pack him some food. He also takes candles, matches, and an oil lantern with him.

By now the trails were easy for him. Stephen moved briskly down the Grand Gallery. He kept the lantern light very low, just bright enough that he wouldn't trip over a rock.

He had never been alone in the cave before, but he wasn't afraid. Somehow he felt welcome in that enormous place.

Very soon he reached Steamboat Rock. He passed through the Wooden Bowl Room and the Deserted Chambers. Just

before the Bottomless Pit lay the object of his quest.
Stephen knelt down beside it, his heart beating fast.

Right here, a crack in the floor led down to a lower level
called the Labyrinth. Archibald Miller had taken Stephen this
way just once. He had told Stephen that "labyrinth" means a
confusing maze. The tunnels on the lower level turned and
twisted. It was easy to get lost, and that was why the tours
never came this way.

Stephen eased his way down into the narrow opening. He
moved carefully. If he dropped the lantern, it might break, and
he had no other. It would be a long, dark journey back to the
mouth of the cave.

But he felt like a real explorer, and he was determined not to be afraid. He had the feeling that some thrilling sight was just waiting to be discovered. He wanted to be the one to discover it.

He eased down out of the crack and found himself standing in a high, narrow passageway. He tried to remember where Archibald Miller had taken him. In one direction lay Bottomless Pit, but there was no way to cross it on this level, either. What was in the other direction?

Stephen thought for a moment. He dared not lose his way. Only Nita knew he was in the cave, and she had no idea where he was exploring. If Stephen got lost, no one would know where to find him.

He had tucked a few candles in with his lunch. He dug one out and lit it from the lantern flame. Then he stuck it into a crack between the rocks on the floor and watched to see if it would blow out.

But this deep inside the cave, there was no wind at all. The little flame burned steadily. With it to mark the place where he had entered the Labyrinth, Stephen felt safe to explore further.

He moved down the tunnel cautiously, making sure to watch the floor in front of him. Now the main tunnel began to branch off in many directions. Stephen ventured a little way down one passageway, but quickly returned.

All these rocky pathways looked the same. Now he understood why this place was called the Labyrinth.

Then he had an idea.

He lit another candle stub. This time he used the smoke from the candle flame to burn a crude arrow onto the wall of the cave. It pointed back the way he had come.

As long as he marked his way back, he would be safe. He went on, holding his lantern high.

The tunnels twisted and turned, but Stephen kept to as straight a path as he could manage. At each intersection he was careful to smoke an arrow pointing back along his trail.

Stephen does find another passage! It leads him to a way to climb down partway into the Bottomless Pit.

Zoom In

Why doesn't Stephen's candle blow out when he is deep inside the cave? What part of the story helped you answer?

He slid carefully down into the pit. There was an opening in the right-hand wall, almost like a window. Stephen thrust his candle into the blackness. What he saw made his eyes widen.

He was looking into a huge vertical shaft. It was like looking *up* into a wide, rocky tunnel. Stephen's light was not bright enough to show either a roof or a floor. But straight across from him was a beautiful sight.

Most of the walls in Mammoth Cave were of gray stone. But this shaftway was beautifully colored. It looked as though an enormous yellow-and-white candle had melted down the curved walls. Streaks of red and black added even more color.

Water dripped across the wall from some unseen source overhead. The wet rock gleamed in the dim light from Stephen's candle.

Stephen was thrilled. Was he the first person ever to see this sight? He would not be the last, that was certain.

Stephen Bishop really lived. He was the first great American cave explorer. He not only found new cave passages but also made the first detailed map of them.

Prove It

What did the beautiful shaftway look like? What details from the story helped you answer?

A Rock's Story

by Dina McClellan

I'll tell you a secret:
I won't always be a rock.
Water is seeping through my cracks,
prying them open,
bit by bit,
slowly
taking me
apart.
The wind is wearing me away, too.
One day I will be sand.
Come see me at the beach!

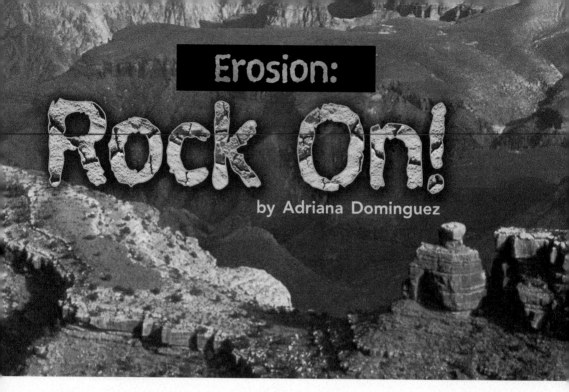

Erosion: Rock On!

by Adriana Dominguez

Scientists think the Grand Canyon was formed by **erosion**. Erosion is a powerful **force** that can change the shape of the land. Erosion is a process with three parts. They are **weathering,** erosion itself, and **deposition**.

Weathering is the breaking down of rocks and soil. Weathering can be caused by wind, heat, water, or ice. Very slowly, rocks break down into smaller pieces. In the Grand Canyon, the Colorado River broke down layers of rock.

Erosion happens when those smaller pieces of broken rock and soil are blown, washed, or carried from one place to another. Wind, water, or gravity can carry away those smaller pieces. In the Grand Canyon, the river washed the small pieces of rock away. This made the deep canyon.

Deposition is when the loose pieces of rock and soil are dropped in a new place. Think of all the bits of rock, soil, and sand in the Colorado River. Every day the river carries them downstream and deposits them in a new place farther down the river. The shape of the land keeps on changing.

wind

heat

water

ice

What Causes Weathering and Erosion?

The wind causes erosion when it picks up sand and soil and blows it around. It can move the sand and soil from place to place, changing the shape of the land.

Sharp changes in heat and cold can cause weathering and erosion. Heat makes rocks expand. Cold makes them get smaller. Over time, these changes crack the rocks. Small pieces can then come loose.

Rivers cause erosion. They wash away sand and soil. They gradually wear down rock. Ocean waves crashing into the **shore** also cause erosion.

Water expands when it freezes into ice. When water in a crack of stone freezes, the expanding ice can break the rock apart!

Prove It

What details in the text show how erosion changes the land?

The Shrinking Truth

by Tomaso Rivera

How do wind and rain change soil?

You don't need a whole river or ocean to cause erosion. Even tiny raindrops can move soil. They can splash small pieces from one place to another. When it rains, flowing water makes tracks called gullies. Each time it rains, the gullies get bigger. The flowing water carries soil down the hill. What do you guess will be the **effect** of raindrops on your pile of dirt? Check your pile during the week for gullies. See if they get bigger when it rains. Share your findings with your classmates.

Materials:
- pile of dirt
- tape measure
- notebook
- pencil

Experiment!

Step 1
Get a pile of dirt. Pack it tightly outdoors.

Step 2
Write down the height and width of your "mountain."

Step 3
Wait one week. Take measurements.

Step 4
Wait another week. Take measurements.

What happened?
Wind and rain make your dirt smaller over time.
This is erosion.

The Andes and the Rockies

by Mia Lewis

The Andes are the longest mountain range in South America. They stretch all the way from the very northern edge to the very southern tip of the continent. That's about 5,500 miles top to bottom. In North America, the longest mountain range is the Rockies. This range is about 3,000 miles long.

The Andes range has many tall peaks higher than 19,000 feet. The highest mountain in the Western Hemisphere, Aconcagua, is in the Andes Mountains. The tallest peaks in the Rockies are only about 14,400 feet high.

The Andes run along the western side of South America. They pass through seven countries: Venezuela, Colombia, Ecuador, Peru, Bolivia, Chile, and Argentina. The Rockies begin in Canada and end in the United States. In the U.S. they pass through

Rocky Mountains

North America

Andes Mountains

South America

the states of Idaho, Montana, Wyoming, Utah, Colorado, and New Mexico.

Both the Andes and the Rockies are popular with hikers and climbers. Both have glaciers. In the Andes there are several active volcanoes! These features all make both ranges very interesting to learn about and to visit.

Prove It

What details show that both the Andes and the Rockies are very long mountain ranges?

Learn the Words

process
canyon
dissolve
layer
cave
effect
alter
shore

- Read the words on the list.
- Read the dialogue.
- Find the words.

The **canyon** looks so deep!

You can see each **layer** of rock.

What is the **effect** of wind on these cliffs?

It can **alter** their shape—in about a million years!

1. Play "Guess Who"
Listening and Speaking

Pick someone in the picture. Have your partner guess whom you chose. Your partner can ask up to five yes-or-no questions first. (It's not fair just to point at each person!) Then change roles with your partner.

2. Class Trip to a Cave
Writing

Would you like to visit an underground cave? Tell why, or why not. Give two reasons. Share your reasons with your partner. Before you start, ask your partner questions about any words you don't understand.

3. You Are the Author
Writing

How would you tell about the place in the picture? Write at least five details. Use them to make a poem. You can look at the poem "A Rock's Story" for ideas. Your poem doesn't have to rhyme! Show the poem to your partner.

4. Take a Survey
Graphic Organizer

Ask 5 classmates what class trip they would choose. Tally their answers in a chart. Share your findings with your partner.

Which Trip?	Number of Votes
a large cave	
a big canyon	
a shore	

The underground Caves of the United States

by Takeshi Ando

Have you ever visited a cave? Caves are a good place to learn about geology and the forces that have shaped Earth.

"Show caves" are set up for tourists. They have lights, stairs, and guides. They even have elevators or trains. In a "wild cave" you might have to crawl, climb, or squeeze through tight passageways. Here are a few of the many amazing caves in the United States.

Carlsbad Cavern, New Mexico

You can take an elevator down to the Big Room. It is one of the largest underground chambers in the world. Or you can walk down 755 feet of a steep and winding path. Water trickling down slowly **dissolved** the soft limestone to create the chambers.

Ape Cave, Washington

This cave is a lava tube. It was made when Mount St. Helens erupted about 1,900 years ago. It is 2.5 miles long. It was explored by a scout troop called the Mount St. Helens Apes. That's probably how the cave got its name.

Niagara Cave, Minnesota

Underground streams formed these caves long ago. They carved a high ceiling with canyons and gorges below. Some of the streams are still flowing. One has a waterfall. The cave even has a special place for weddings! It also has a spot where visitors can dig for precious stones.

Mammoth Cave, Kentucky

Mammoth is filled with incredible rock formations and deep caverns. People have been exploring the caves for a long time. More than 50 kinds of animals live in the cave. One mile inside the cave, scientists found remains from American Indians dating back about 4,000 years.

Mammoth Cave National Park!

Click on the links for more information about the park:

- Home Page
- History of the Park
- Geology
- Plants and Animals
- Fun Facts for Kids
- In the News
- Photo Gallery
- Support Mammoth Cave
- Español

Mammoth Cave National Park was created in 1941. The purpose was to protect the amazing caves underground and the land above them. The park also protects the many special animals that live in the caves.

Mammoth Cave, Kentucky is the longest cave system in the world! It is not just one cave, but a system of many connected caves. About 400 miles of the cave have been explored. But new caves and passages are explored every year.

The caves and caverns inside Mammoth Cave were formed in underground limestone. Water dissolved the limestone, leaving empty spaces behind. Too many visitors or too much pollution can have a bad effect on Mammoth Cave. The park rangers work hard to protect the caves, the land around them, and all the plants and animals.

Visitors to Mammoth Cave can go on many different tours. Some are easy and some are hard! Pick one that fits your skill level. Click on the "Preparing for Your Tour" link for tips on what to wear and what to expect.

Click on these links to plan your visit:

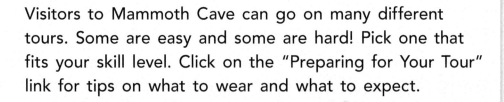

GO Maps and Directions

GO Where to Stay

GO Local Weather

GO Tour Information

GO Preparing for Your Tour

GO Contact Us

Where to Stay

Cave City Campground 555-4063
Located close to Mammoth Cave.

Kentucky Inn 555-9915
Beautiful views! Swimming pool.

Retell "Stronger Than Rock"

> ℹ️ When you retell a story, you can give the causes of the most important events. This helps readers understand why things happen in a story. You can use words such as *if, then, because, due to,* and *therefore* to tell about causes and effects.

"Stronger Than Rock" is realistic fiction. It tells about several forces that made the Grand Canyon so big. Review the selection on pages 116–119. Look at the pictures on page 141.

◼ First Cause: What is it? How did it cause erosion?

◼ Second and Third Causes: What did wind and the Colorado River do?

◼ Effect: Describe how the rock changed because of those forces.

Use the pictures on page 141 to retell the selection to your partner. As you give each cause, and then the effect, point to the correct picture. Use complete sentences.

Words you might use in your retelling:

erosion	weathering	force
cliff	process	break down

cause

cause

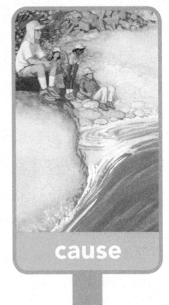

cause

effect

Dig Deeper

Look Back

Work with a partner. Decide what details you could use to prove or support each statement below. Write one detail for each statement. Tell the page number where you found that piece of evidence.

- Ice can change rock by breaking a rock apart.

- River guides on the Colorado River need to learn how to do their job right.

- Glaciers are made of snow and ice.

Talk About It

What would be good questions to ask a guide on the Colorado River? Work with a partner. Use what you have read in this unit. Come up with four questions. They do not have to be questions that are already answered in the selections.

If any of your questions can be answered from the unit, work with your partner to answer them.

Conversation

 Use the words *should, must,* or *have to* to tell about things that someone needs to do. When you tell someone to do something, be polite. Thank the person who does what you say.

Talk to a partner. One of you will be person A. The other will be person B.

Person A

Tell your partner to do a task.

Reply.

Reply.

Person B

Reply. Ask a question about the task.

Ask your partner for help.

Thank your partner.

UNEARTHING *the Past*

The **BIG** Question

Why do we study the past? How can we learn from it?

☐ What can scientists find out when they study fossils?

☐ What animals lived long ago but aren't around now?

☐ Which animals look a lot like animals that lived long ago?

What do we learn from studying the past?

1. What animals lived long ago?

Millions of years ago, Earth was home to…

- ☐ birds.

- ☐ dinosaurs.

- ☐ other reptiles.

- ☐ mammals.

2. What can fossils teach us?

We can learn…

- ☐ what extinct animals looked like.

- ☐ which prehistoric animals are still around.

- ☐ how today's animals are related to extinct animals.

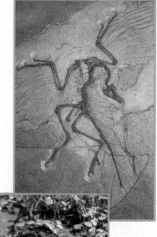

3. How can we learn more about fossils?

People can...

☐ look at a museum exhibit.

☐ visit a dig site.

☐ learn science at school.

☐ study what others have discovered.

4. Why do people study extinct animals?

People study extinct animals...

☐ to compare them with today's animals.

☐ to learn what Earth was like long ago.

☐ to find out what animals once lived in their region.

Say **more!**

Learn the Words

extinct
prehistoric
bone
fossil
paleontologist
identify
skeleton
exhibit

Theme Vocabulary

The easiest way to remember the meaning of a new word is to use the word. As you discuss ways that people unearth the past, use these vocabulary words. Use them when you read and write about unearthing the past, too.

Read the word.
Look at the picture.
Listen to your teacher.

extinct

prehistoric

bone

fossil

paleontologist

identify

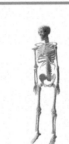

skeleton

exhibit

Which Picture?

Look at the vocabulary cards. Choose one picture. Don't tell anyone what it is! Describe the picture. See if your partner can guess which picture you chose.

SCIENCE FAIR

 Mr. Grimm   **Mr. Grant**   **Carlos** The Skink

1. Today is the school's Science Fair.

2. The competition is stiff...

CARLOS'S SKINK

3. ... but I'm going to knock everyone's socks off!

Hey Carlos, what do you have there?

Is that a skunk?

It's a—

5 No, it's not a—

Look everyone, Carlos brought a skunk to class!

6 A skunk?

There's a skunk in the class!

7 What's all this about a skunk?

8 Carlos has a skunk in a box!

But I—

9 Carlos, why did you bring a skunk to my class?

I didn't, Mr. Grant. Let me show you…

10 Don't you dare open that box! You'll stink up the whole room!

3 Formal/Informal Language To "knock someone's socks off" means to "surprise and amaze" the person. Is this expression formal or informal?

151

ℹ️ 12 13 **Formal/Informal Language** When Carlos talks to Mr. Grimm, does he use informal language? Why or why not?

It's like a snake, but with legs. And it doesn't stink at all!

I've never seen anything like it before.

Carlos, I owe you an apology.

Class, we jumped to the wrong conclusion.

Carlos did not bring a skunk. He brought a skink. And he's going to tell us all about it.

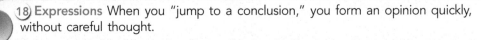

18 **Expressions** When you "jump to a conclusion," you form an opinion quickly, without careful thought.

DIAGRAM THE BONES

by Max Corbin

Fossils are the remains of plants or animals that lived long, long ago. Fossils can be **bones**, teeth, eggs, nests, footprints, or parts of plants. Most fossils are from types of animals that are no longer alive today.

It is hard to know what Earth was like millions of years ago. Studying fossils gives us clues. Fossils are like puzzle pieces from the past. When we put the pieces together, we get a clearer picture of life on Earth long ago.

The scientists who study fossils are called **paleontologists**. They can get a lot of information from a fossil. Fossils tell them how animals have changed over time. Fossils show how different animals are **related** to each other.

Fossils are not always easy to find. Many are **buried** under rock and soil. Sometimes they are very deep inside the earth.

Paleontologists dig for fossils very carefully. The place where paleontologists dig is called a dig **site**. They draw a diagram of the site. This diagram shows the dig site pictured on page 154.

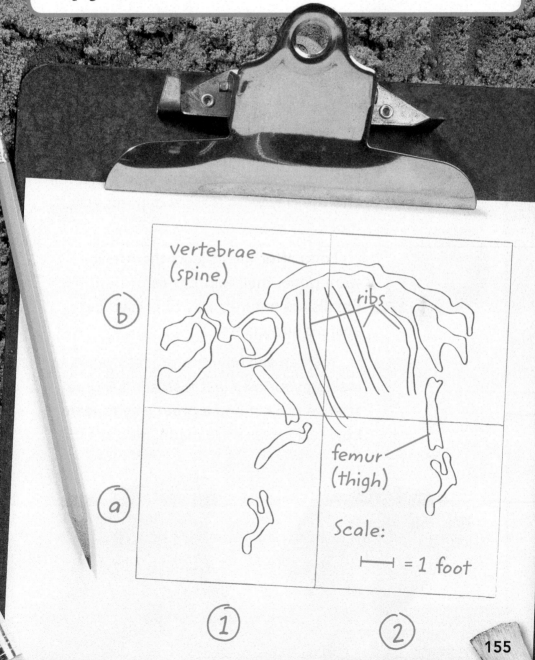

vertebrae (spine)

ribs

femur (thigh)

Scale:

⊢—⊣ = 1 foot

b

a

1

2

Procedural Text

How To Make a Leaf Fossil

by Sean Williams

The first fossils were made millions of years ago when animals ran across wet clay that later hardened into rock. Feathers, leaves, and other items that fell into the clay were fossilized in this way, too.

Long after the objects themselves were gone, their imprints remained. Fossils are nature's way of preserving animals and plants.

You can see how this process works by making your own leaf fossils. It's a great science project and a great way to learn how real fossils were made. Plus, it's fun!

As you work, think about how your leaves could have landed in the wet clay on their own.

Here's What You'll Need

a plastic ice cube tray   petroleum jelly

clear glue   toothpicks

leaves

Step 1: Rub some petroleum jelly into the cups of the ice cube tray.

Step 2: Pour some clear glue into each cup.

Step 3: Use toothpicks to press the leaves into the glue.

Step 4: Wait a few days for the glue to dry.

Step 5: Take out the cubes and admire your very own fossils!

Rhinos
Then and Now
by Ivan Grinkov

The woolly rhino and the white rhino are two kinds of rhinoceros. They are similar in many ways, but they are also different. Let's **compare**!

The woolly rhino was covered with thick, shaggy brown hair. The white rhino, on the other hand, has almost no hair. Even though it is called the "white" rhino, it is actually gray in color.

Apart from their hair, woolly rhinos and white rhinos look alike in many ways. The woolly rhino stood about six feet high. It had short, thick legs and two horns. The front horn was flat from side to side. The white rhino also stands about six feet high. It has short, thick legs, and two horns. The difference is that both of the white rhino's horns are rounded.

The biggest difference between these two kinds of rhinos is that one is alive today, and the other is not. The woolly rhino has been **extinct** for about 10,000 years! The white rhino is still living. While the woolly rhino was alive, it roamed Europe and Asia. Today, the white rhino lives in Africa.

	Woolly	White
Range	Europe and Asia	Africa
Hair	long, shaggy, brown hair	almost hairless body
Horn	two horns, the front one flat from side to side	two horns, both rounded
Height	about 6 feet high at the shoulders	about 6 feet high at the shoulders
Legs	short, thick legs	short, thick legs
Food	plant-eater	plant-eater
Lived	extinct 10,000 years ago	still living today

Scientists know about the woolly rhino from remains found in the snow and ice of Siberia. Fossils of the woolly rhino help scientists learn about where it lived and what it looked like.

Living Fossils

by Mia Lewis

Most life forms on Earth change slowly over time. They change in order to be more successful at staying alive. But a few plants and animals do not change. They have stayed almost exactly the same for millions of years. They don't need to change because they are doing just fine!

Living fossils are the rare animals and plants that have survived since **prehistoric** times without much change. Many of them seem odd or unusual. That's because they do not have many close relatives.

The nautilus has a shell with many closed spaces filled with gas and liquid. The nautilus uses these spaces to control how much it floats or sinks under the water.

The duck-billed platypus is a very strange and mixed-up animal. It is a mammal, but it lays eggs. It has a bill like a duck, a tail like a beaver, and feet like an otter. Stingers on its back feet are filled with poison.

Hoatzin chicks are born with claws on the ends of their wings. They use the claws to climb up trees before they can fly. They lose these claws when they grow up.

The tuatara looks like a lizard, but it is in a group all its own. It can live to be 80 or 100 years old. It has a strange "third eye" on top of its head.

Hagfish are not exactly fish. They are in their own category. They have two brains, one **skull**, and no backbone. When these creatures are upset, they produce a thick slime that protects them from predators.

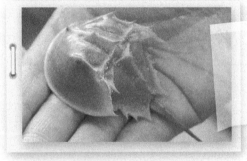

The horseshoe crab has been around since before there were dinosaurs. The horseshoe crab is more closely related to spiders than it is to other crabs.

Prove It

What detail helps you know that there are not a lot of other animals that look like these?

SHARKS!

by Susan Guthrie and Mia Lewis

How long have sharks been swimming in the seas? These large fish may have been around for over 400 million years!

Sharks do not have bones like other fish. Instead, they have cartilage. The wiggly bit at the end of your nose is cartilage. It is more flexible and lighter than bone. The problem for paleontologists is that cartilage doesn't turn into fossil the way bone does. The only parts of a shark that make good fossils are its teeth.

Scientists have **discovered** very old shark teeth. Some are 400 million years old. These fossil teeth are a lot like the teeth of today's sharks. Sharks haven't changed much in a long time!

great white shark

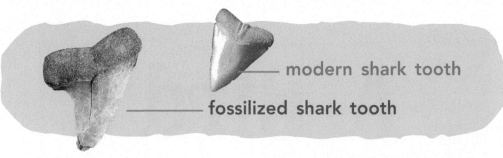

—— modern shark tooth

—— fossilized shark tooth

Sharks are strong, fast, and deadly hunters. They can open their jaws very wide to attack their prey. They have lots of sharp teeth. Some sharks have teeth arranged in rows. Imagine five or six rows of shark teeth! Shark teeth fall out all the time and are replaced by new ones.

Today there are more than 350 kinds of sharks. New ones are discovered every year. The largest shark in the world is the whale shark. It grows up to 40 or 50 feet long. But this big shark is not dangerous to people. It eats only tiny creatures! The smallest shark in the world is the dwarf dogshark. It is 7 inches long or less when it is fully grown.

hammerhead shark

nurse shark

A Bird Fossil Expert

by Marilee Robin Burton

A Pioneer of Science

Hildegarde Howard loved old bird bones. She spent her whole life studying them. Dr. Howard was a bird paleontologist. She was the first woman to do this job.

To Dr. Howard, bird bones told stories about the past. Fossils are rarely found whole. Paleontologists have to fit tiny bone pieces together to make a complete animal fossil. Then they can see what the animal looked like. Dr. Howard was especially good at fitting fossil pieces together. To her, they were like pieces of a puzzle. She tried to fit them together. When she fit fossils together, they taught her secrets about the past.

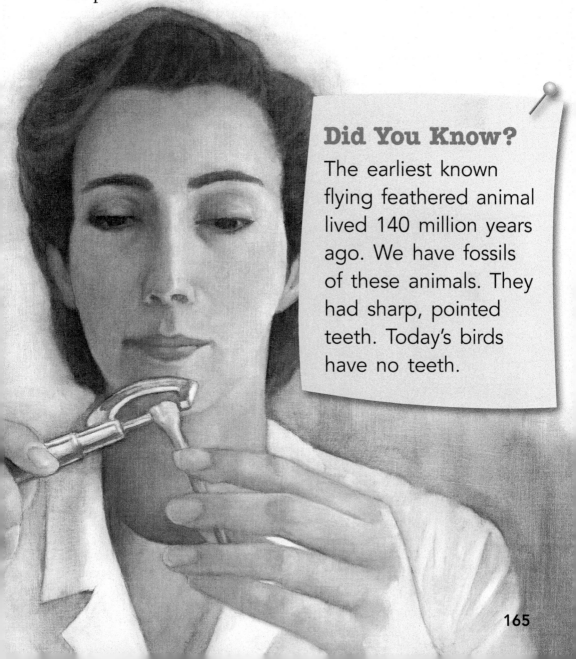

Did You Know?

The earliest known flying feathered animal lived 140 million years ago. We have fossils of these animals. They had sharp, pointed teeth. Today's birds have no teeth.

Inspired by a Teacher

At first, Hildegarde Howard wanted to be a newspaper writer. She hardly knew what a fossil was! Then she took a science course in college. Science amazed her. She decided to become a scientist. She was able to get a part-time job with a paleontologist, Chester Stock. Now she was on her way to a career as a fossil expert.

Becoming a scientist wasn't easy for a woman in those days. Female students were not even allowed on field trips! However, Hildegarde Howard earned three science degrees. Now she was Dr. Howard, a paleontologist.

Birds from the Past

Dr. Howard's first job was at the Natural History Museum of Los Angeles. Her task was sorting bones. She helped to clean, **identify**, and **classify** bones.

Bird fossils interested her the most. One extinct bird she studied was the California turkey. She looked at 800 California turkey bones.

A Career Woman

Dr. Howard was born in 1901 in Washington, DC. In 1920, she started college. At that time, few women went to college. Most people thought that women should only be wives and mothers.

Zoom In

What detail shows why Hildegarde Howard changed her mind about what job she would do?

Years of Discovery

Dr. Howard discovered many unknown prehistoric birds. One of these was the bony-toothed bird. She named many of the birds.

Much of Dr. Howard's work took place at the La Brea Tar Pits. The La Brea Tar Pits are in California. They are one of the world's richest fossil sites.

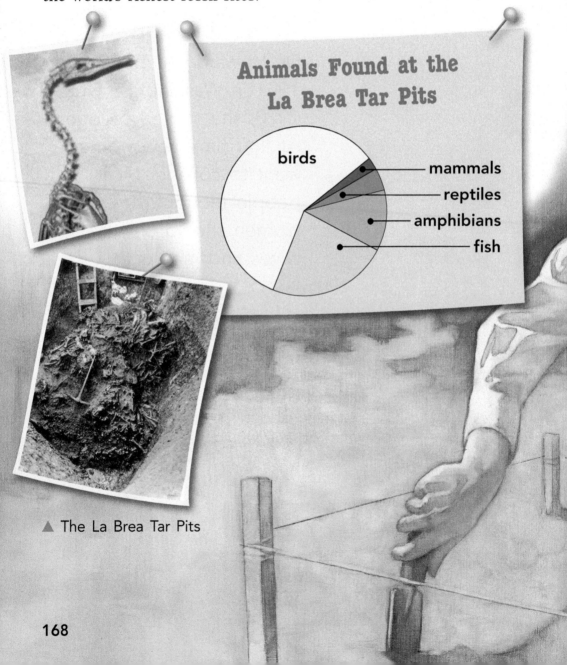

Animals Found at the La Brea Tar Pits

birds

mammals

reptiles

amphibians

fish

▲ The La Brea Tar Pits

A Leader in Her Field

Dr. Howard was in charge of building bird **skeletons**. She wanted the skeletons to look real for museum visitors. Her ideas changed the way museums presented fossils.

Dr. Howard stopped working in 1961. She didn't stop studying birds, though. She continued until she died in 1991. The museum wanted to honor Dr. Howard. An **exhibit** hall was named after her.

What was the secret to her success? She loved her work!

Prove It

Dr. Howard compared fossils to puzzle pieces. In what way are they like puzzle pieces?

My Journal

by Melody Tranha

KEEP Out!

Monday, March 3

I've been thinking a lot about the job I want when I grow up. It's hard because I like so many things. It would be great to be able to work part of the time outdoors and part indoors. I love doing puzzles and building things. What kind of job mixes indoors and outdoors, puzzles, and building? I have no idea!

In social studies we found out we have to do a report on a person. I'm trying to think of a person to write about. It could be an explorer or a builder, or maybe someone who does puzzles.

I'm not looking forward to tomorrow. We have a double science period in the afternoon.

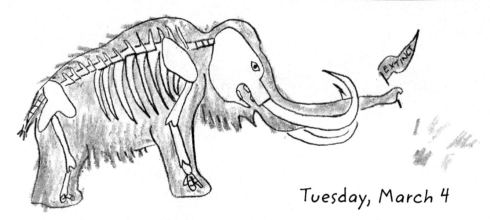

Tuesday, March 4

My double science period turned out to be fun. We learned about fossils and paleontologists. It's amazing how many extinct animals there are. The only way to learn about them is to find and study fossils of their bones and teeth.

Paleontologists have a funny job. They spend part of their time digging for buried fossils. They spend the rest of their time studying the fossils. They identify and classify the bones and label them carefully. When the paleontologists compare the bones they find with other bones, they can see how different kinds of animals are related.

Tomorrow we are going on a field trip to the Page Museum at the La Brea Tar Pits. The museum is right in the city of Los Angeles.

Wednesday, March 5

I just got back from my field trip! The La Brea Tar Pits are a place where tar has been seeping up from the ground for thousands of years. Animals got trapped, and then the tar kept their bones from falling apart. It's amazing! Over the years, scientists have found more than a million fossils here.

I loved the skeletons of the giant California Condor. We also saw a camel, a mammoth, a saber-toothed cat, and skulls from the dire wolf.

One really amazing thing at the museum is the "Fishbowl Lab." It's a real lab where scientists are busy identifying bones. They have to classify them and label them carefully. They compare bones to see which animals are related. Volunteers work in the Fishbowl as well. Maybe I can volunteer some day.

Thursday, March 6

One of the people we learned about yesterday was Hildegarde Howard. I think I'm going to do my report on her.

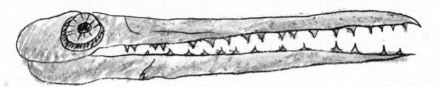

Howard was a paleontologist. She did lots of work at the La Brea Tar Pits site. She was interested in bird fossils. She discovered a prehistoric bird that no one had found before. Hildegarde Howard was amazing.

Hildegarde Howard worked outside, digging up buried bones and fossils. She worked inside identifying, classifying, comparing, and labeling what she found. Putting the bones together to make skeletons was like doing a puzzle.

I know what job I should do! I should be a paleontologist. That way I'll get to work outside and inside. I'll get to build things and do puzzles. If I find a good site full of fossils, maybe I will discover a new prehistoric animal! I hope it has lots of teeth.

Prove It

What was the most important effect that the field trip had on the writer of the journal? What evidence supports this?

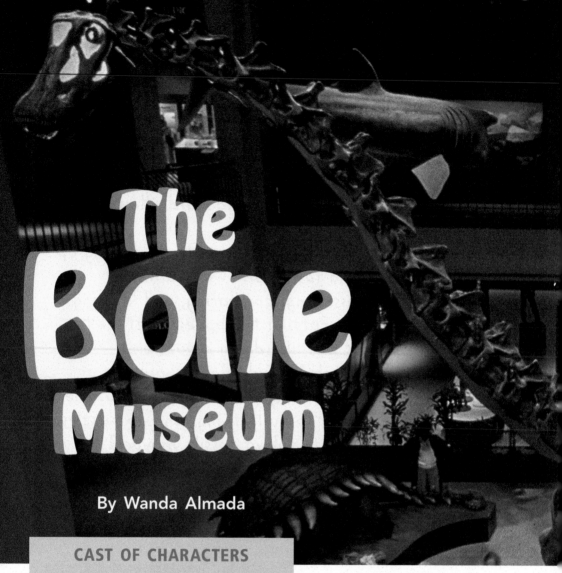

The Bone Museum

By Wanda Almada

CAST OF CHARACTERS

DR. PONCE, a paleontologist

ALICIA, Dr. Ponce's daughter

NANDO, Alicia's friend

The setting is a workroom in a natural history museum on a Sunday afternoon. The museum is closed. ALICIA and NANDO are entering the workroom. A man seated at a worktable looks up to greet them.

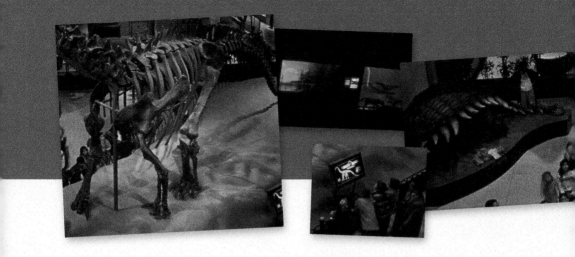

DR. PONCE: Come in, Alicia! Very happy to see you. Won't you introduce me to your friend?

ALICIA: Yes, Papa. This is Nando, my friend from school. Nando, this is my dad, Dr. Ponce.

NANDO: Hi. (*looking around*) Alicia said you worked in a museum. I thought she meant one with, you know, *paintings*!

DR. PONCE: Oh no! Alicia, can you explain?

ALICIA: This is a natural history museum. It tells about the history of the earth—animals, plants, rocks, and everything! My dad works on exhibits that show extinct animals.

NANDO: Hmm. But, what's with all the bones? Isn't that kind of, well, creepy?

DR. PONCE: Not at all! You see, fossilized bones are all we have left of animals that are extinct. Looking at the bones tells us a lot about these animals.

NANDO: Some of the skeletons out in the exhibits are kind of cool, I guess. But back here it's just dinosaur bones scattered everywhere!

> **Zoom In**
>
> Where does "The Bone Museum" take place?

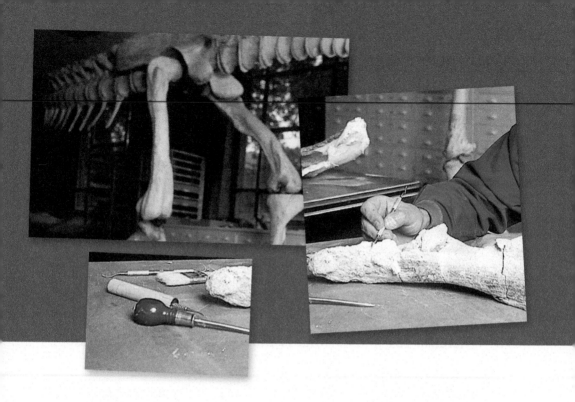

ALICIA: No, Nando! (*giggling a little*) These aren't dinosaur bones. There were also mammals millions of years ago. These are all mammal bones. My dad works on mammals.

DR. PONCE: This workroom is where we study the bones. Some of them are millions of years old! It's my job to figure out which ones go together. (*pointing*) See, right now I'm working on putting together the bones of an early form of horse. In fact, I have to get back to work. You kids go look at the exhibits. Come back when you have found the animal you think has changed the most over the years, and the one you think has changed the least.

NANDO: (*as they leave the workroom, sounding bored*) I don't get it. Why would the animals be different or the same? Do we have to search?

ALICIA: Come on! This could be fun. Take a look over here. This woolly mammoth is like an elephant, but back then it was very hairy. I think the woolly mammoth had this shaggy fur to stay warm. It lived long ago when Earth was icy cold.

NANDO: Wow! That *is* a big change! This is the coolest elephant I've ever seen!

ALICIA: Yea, pretty cool. Or do you mean warm? (*giggles*) But look at this. Here's a crocodile. What do you think? Has it changed much?

NANDO: Wait, is this the old one or one from today?

ALICIA: You can't tell, right? This crocodile is from the time of the dinosaurs, but it looks just the same as crocodiles look today. It's hardly changed at all.

NANDO: Weird! What's over here? Is that a bear or a cow? It has a big tail and such big teeth.

ALICIA: Check it out. It's a giant beaver! Back then beavers were much larger than beavers today. They were up to eight feet long and they weighed 200 pounds.

NANDO: That's a scary beaver. It's so strange that today's beavers are smaller. Did other animals change size like that?

ALICIA: I think wolves used to be much bigger also. Let's take a look around and see what we can find. (*pointing*) You go that way and I'll go this way. I'll meet you back at the workroom in 30 minutes.

(The two students go off in separate directions, looking at the exhibits as they go. Later they meet back at the workroom.)

DR. PONCE: Well? What did you find? First, what animal has changed the least?

ALICIA: I say the crocodile. Am I right, Papa?

NANDO: What about the horseshoe crab?

DR. PONCE: Well done, both of you. Yes, the crocodile has stayed much the same for millions of years. But the horseshoe crab has been unchanged even longer. Now, which animal did you find that has changed the most?

ALICIA: Is it the beaver? It's so much smaller now than it used to be.

NANDO: It's the horse! Early horses were tiny. They were the size of a small dog.

DR. PONCE: You're right, Nando! Take a look. I've got the skeleton put together here. Now all I need to do is add this small skull, and it is ready to gallop off to its exhibit. So, how do you like the museum without paintings?

NANDO: It's awesome! I'm coming back tomorrow when the museum is open!

Prove It

What details of "The Bone Museum" let you know that it is a play?

Learn the Words

classify
skull
site
discover
buried
compare
related
label

- Read the words on the list.
- Read the dialogue.
- Find the words.

We were digging up a 2,000-year-old city. Then we found prehistoric animal bones **buried** here.

That's why we invited paleontologists to the **site**.

1. Be the Writer
Writing

Pretend that you are at a dig site like the one in the picture. You discover the bones of a prehistoric animal. Write a journal entry. Tell what happens. Tell how you feel. Show your journal entry to your partner.

2. Make a Chart
Graphic Organizer

Name as many animals as you can. Classify them as birds, reptiles, mammals, or "other." Write each one in the correct row. Share the chart with your partner.

Birds	
Reptiles	
Mammals	
Other	

I hear they found a bird's **skull** this morning.

What else will they **discover** here?

Let's **compare** them to the bones I found. They could be **related.**

I will **classify** the bones I found. I'll put a **label** on each bone.

3. You Are the Actor
Listening and Speaking

Work with a partner. Ask your partner questions about any word you don't understand. Then take turns reading the dialogue in the picture. Use your best acting voice. Make the dialogue come alive.

4. Make an Ad
Listening and Speaking

Suppose you are in charge of a prehistoric dig site. You need workers! Make an ad to get workers to join you. Show your ad to your partner. Share your ideas.

Can You

I'm a paleontologist,
And I've come to say,
You can learn about the past by
digging today.

Many special things
Are buried underground.

Fossils and bones are
Just waiting to be found.

Can you dig it?

These clues to the past
Tell us a lot
About life long ago
In a particular spot.

Can you dig it?

Dig It?

by Katie Sharp

To uncover these clues,
A place must be found
Where prehistoric beasts
May have roamed around.

Can you dig it?

You'll use special tools
To unearth the past.
Digging deep, deeper, deepest
Till you finish your task.

Can you dig it?

Application for Summer Paleontology Camp

Name of Camper:

_____

First   Middle   Last

Parents' or Guardians' Names

_____

First   Middle   Last

_____

First   Middle   Last

How old will you be in September?

_____

Age   Grade

What is your address?

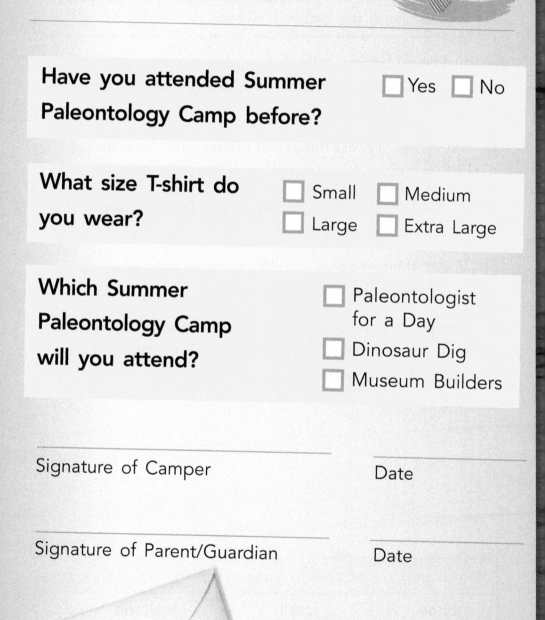

What school do you attend?

_____

Have you attended Summer Paleontology Camp before?
☐ Yes ☐ No

What size T-shirt do you wear?
☐ Small ☐ Medium
☐ Large ☐ Extra Large

Which Summer Paleontology Camp will you attend?
☐ Paleontologist for a Day
☐ Dinosaur Dig
☐ Museum Builders

_____   _____

Signature of Camper   Date

_____   _____

Signature of Parent/Guardian   Date

Retell "A Bird Fossil Expert"

When you retell a selection, you tell only the most important events. Tell the events in order. Use words such as *first, next,* and *then.* This will help readers understand the order of events.

"A Bird Fossil Expert" tells about events in one person's life. Review the selection on pages 164–169. Look at the four pictures on page 187.

■ First Picture: What important events took place during the first part of the selection?

■ Second Picture: What important events took place in this part of the selection?

■ Third and Fourth Pictures: What events took place in the selection's last two parts?

Use the pictures on page 187 to retell the selection to your partner. As you retell each event, point to the correct picture. Use complete sentences.

Words you might use in your retelling:

bone	fossil	skeleton
identify	discover	exhibit

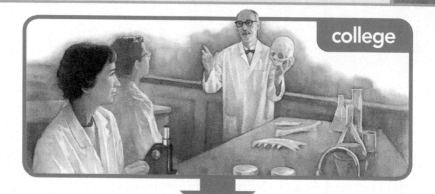

college

studying birds

discoveries

influence

Dig Deeper

Look Back

Find at least three charts or diagrams in the unit.
On a sheet of paper, do these things:

1. Tell what page each chart or diagram is on.

2. Tell one fact you learned from each chart or diagram.

3. Tell which animal or animals each chart or diagram shows.

Talk About It

If you could go back in time, what extinct
animal would you like to see?

Would you like to see dinosaurs?
How about birds or fish?

Write about your choice.

Do you agree with your
classmates? Why or why not?

If not, how could you convince others
to change their minds? How could
someone else convince you?

Conversation

 It's fun to discuss what you like and dislike. Use words, but also show your feelings in your face. Remember—be polite if you disagree with someone else.

Talk to a partner. One of you will be person A. The other will be person B.

Person A

Tell about something you like.

Agree or disagree. Tell about something you dislike.

Agree or disagree. Ask what else your partner likes.

Person B

Agree or disagree. Tell about something you like.

Agree or disagree. Tell about something you dislike.

Answer your partner.

THE EARLY AMERICAS

The **BIG** Question

How does going to a new place change you? How can you change the place?

☐ What civilizations existed in North America before the explorers came?

☐ What happened to some of these civilizations through time?

☐ What can we learn from these early civilizations?

191

1. **What was the life of Central American and South American Indians like long ago?**

Long ago, native peoples…

☐ had traditions that were important to them.

☐ belonged to many groups and cultures.

☐ sometimes built great cities.

2. **How did Europeans cause conflict in the Americas?**

People from Europe…

☐ took riches from native peoples.

☐ claimed the lands for themselves.

☐ began wars with Central American and South American Indians.

☐ killed rulers and other people.

3. **What things were part of Mayan culture?**

   The Maya knew how to...

   ☐ make an accurate calendar.

   ☐ use numbers and math.

   ☐ study the stars.

   ☐ make tall stone buildings.

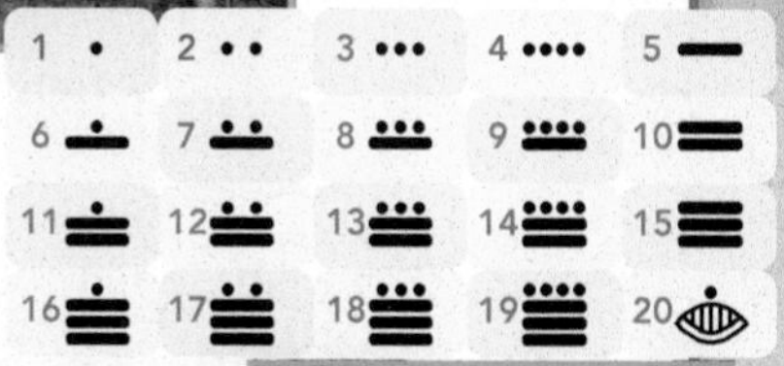

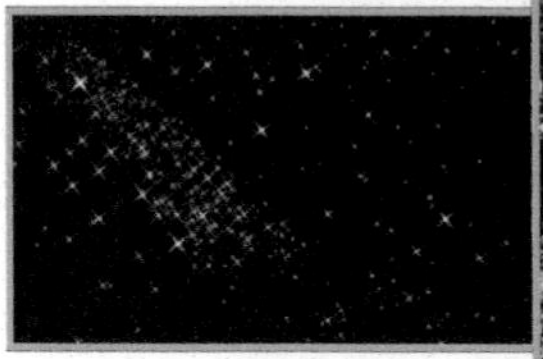

4. **What changes happened because of the conquistadors?**

   The conquistadors...

   ☐ conquered the Aztecs and other peoples.

   ☐ taught native peoples Spanish customs.

   ☐ learned about new foods from native peoples.

   ☐ built new cities on the ruins of native peoples' cities.

   Say **more!**

Theme Vocabulary

Native American
explorer
custom
culture
territory
soldier
ancestor
ruins

The easiest way to remember the meaning of a new word is to use the word. As you discuss the early history of the Americas, use these vocabulary words. Use them when you read and write about the Americas, too.

Read the word.
Look at the picture.
Listen to your teacher.

Native American

explorer

custom

culture

territory

soldier

ancestor

ruins

Match the Pictures

Look at the pictures on the vocabulary cards. Choose two pictures that go together. Tell why you think the pictures go together.

A Deal Is a Deal

Hugo

Pip

Lee

Javier

So Pip, what should we make for lunch today?

Mom said I can use whatever I want.

So let's get creative!

We'll slice up this hard-boiled egg…

Tuna fish always hits the spot.

…and throw in some red jam and cream cheese.

11) **Formal/Informal Language** "What's up?" is an informal way to greet someone and ask what he or she is doing. Would you use this expression to greet an adult you are meeting for the first time?

Just a little something I whipped up.

It's a tuna sandwich with all the trimmings.

Sounds tasty.

13

14

Want to trade?

What do you have?

Ham and cheese.

Okay. You've got a deal.

15

Wait a second....

16

I thought you said this was tuna.

It is!

17

But it's got a lot of other stuff on it.

18

13 **Formal/Informal Language** To "whip up" something means "to make something quickly, without a lot of planning or preparation." Is this formal or informal language?

19 **Formal/Informal Language** How could you say "It's totally gross!" in more formal language?

Many native **cultures** existed in the Americas before European **explorers** arrived. The three most important civilizations were the Maya, the Incas, and the Aztecs.

The Maya lived in Central America, in the Yucatán Peninsula and beyond. When the Maya were strongest, they lived in beautiful cities built of stone. One important Mayan city was Tikal.

The Inca **Empire** stretched more than 2,000 miles along the west coast of South America. The Inca built cities of stone high up in the mountains. Cusco became the **capital** of the Inca Empire. Machu Picchu was another city.

The Aztec lived in Mexico. They began to build their beautiful city Tenochtitlán in 1345. The city became the center of a powerful empire. The Aztec civilization fell to **conquistadors** in 1519.

Mayan statue ▶

▲ Aztec **ruins**

Incan wall ▶
at Cusco

THEY LIVE?

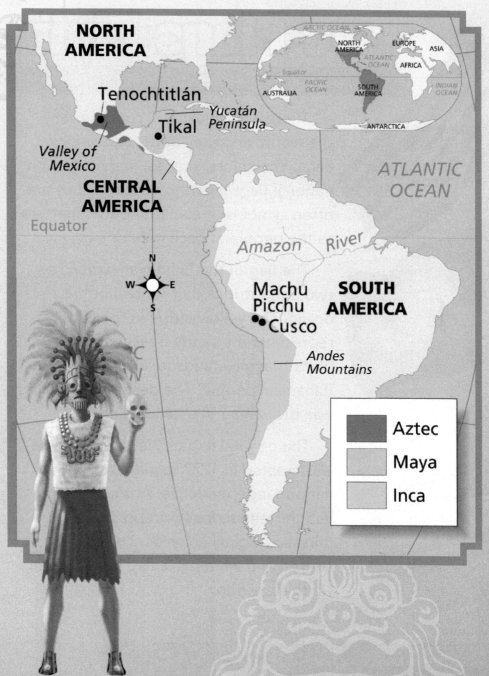

NORTH AMERICA

Tenochtitlán

Yucatán Peninsula

Tikal

Valley of Mexico

CENTRAL AMERICA

Equator

Amazon River

Machu Picchu
Cusco

SOUTH AMERICA

Andes Mountains

ATLANTIC OCEAN

ARCTIC OCEAN

NORTH AMERICA

EUROPE

ASIA

ATLANTIC OCEAN

AFRICA

Equator

PACIFIC OCEAN

AUSTRALIA

SOUTH AMERICA

INDIAN OCEAN

ANTARCTICA

Aztec

Maya

Inca

Two Flags Flying

by Samori Leeds

There are almost 200 countries in the world, and they all have their own flags. The colors, shapes, and images on national flags mean something. They are often symbols of something that matters to the people of each nation.

The flag of the Bahamian nation has two aqua stripes that represent the ocean. The yellow stripe in the middle represents the sandy beaches. The black triangle stands for the unity of the Bahamian people. The design for this flag was the winner in a national contest.

The original flag of the United States was created in 1777 to mark the new nation's independence. At that time it had thirteen stripes to represent the thirteen original colonies. The stripes are red and white. This flag had thirteen white stars, too.

Now we have 50 states, and there are 50 stars on our flag. The colors have meaning. Red is for courage, white is for purity, and blue is for justice.

Rules about how to handle national flags are very strict, no matter whose flag you're talking about.

Here are some rules for handling the flag of the United States:

The U.S. flag should be raised quickly and lowered slowly. It should never be allowed to touch the ground. It is flown at half-staff to show respect for someone who has died. It should not be worn as clothing or to advertise a product. Emergencies are signaled by flying the flag upside down.

Mayan Math

The Maya civilization in Central America developed an advanced number system. They used it to do complicated math.

One difference between Mayan math and our own today is how they wrote their numbers. They used only three symbols: the shell, the dot, and the bar. The shell was used to show the number 0. The dot shows the number 1 and the bar the number 5. Using just these three symbols, they could write any number.

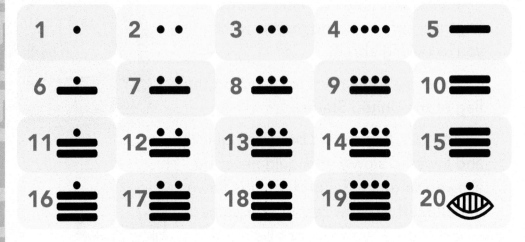

A second difference is that while our math is based on the number 10, Mayan math was based on the number 20. In a two-digit number, we count the number of tens and the number of ones. So 56 equals 5 tens and 6 ones. The Maya would show 56 by writing 2 twenties and 16 ones.

How to Read Mayan Numbers

Read the number from bottom to top.

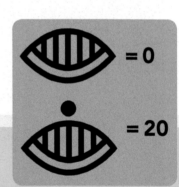

= 20

= 16

20 + 20 + 16 = 56

A. + = ?

B. ••• + = ?

= 0

= 20

Fun Facts

> The Maya figured out
the idea of zero.

> The Mayan system counts
by 20 instead of 10.

Answer Key

A. (6 + 8 = 14)   B. (3 + 9 = 12)

MAYAN

by Elvira Vasquez

Calendars were very important to the Maya. The calendars tracked and predicted the cycles of the Sun, Moon, and stars. The Maya used their calendars to record history. They used them to choose days to perform religious ceremonies, plant crops, and go to war.

▲ A Mayan calendar

CALENDARS

The Maya invented and used several calendars. Each calendar kept track of a different cycle of time: there was a 260-day cycle, a 365-day cycle, a 584-day cycle, and others. Some were used for short periods of time, and others were used for long periods. It took a lot of complicated math to figure out how these calendars fit together.

More than 2,000 years ago, the Maya invented a calendar with 365 days. This was called the Haab calendar. It was based on the cycle of Earth and the Sun. Using the cycle of the Sun is the same way Europeans figured out a 365-day calendar.

Unlike the European 12-month calendar, the Mayan Haab calendar had 18 months. Each month had 20 days. There was a different symbol for each day name. The calendar also had a short month of just 5 days at the end to make the number of days add up to 365. The Maya thought those 5 extra days were unlucky.

Mayan Song of the Earth

adapted from the *Popul Vuh* (1554–1558),
an ancient Mayan text

Measured is the time when we can
Praise the splendor of the earth.

Measured is the time when we can
Know the kindness of the sun.

Measured is the time when the blanket
Of the stars looks down upon us.

And through time, the shadows,
Living within the stars,
Keep watch over their safety
And take measure of their fate.

An Ancient Aztec Poem

adapted from a translation by
Daniel G. Brinton, 1890

Truly as I walk along
I hear the rocks
As if they are replying to the
   sweet songs of the flowers

The glittering, chattering water answers,
The bird-green fountain,
There it sings,
It dashes forth,
It sings again

The mockingbird answers,
Perhaps the coyol bird answers
And many sweet singing birds scatter
   their songs around like music.

They bless the earth pouring out their
   sweet voices.

Sailing with Cortés

The Journal of a Soldier in Cortés's Army

by Jared Matt Greenberg

Hernando Cortés

February 10, 1519

I always dreamed of adventure, and now I am on a real one. We set sail for the Yucatán Peninsula today. I may never see my home again. We are on our way to the mainland of America.

Our leader is Hernando Cortés. He has heard of a land called Mexico that is full of gold. Cortés plans to claim this place for our country, Spain. Can these stories about a land of gold be true?

March 25, 1519

We are on land at last. We have already **encountered** one group. They are Tabascans. From them, we learned that the Aztecs rule this place. The Aztec empire is rich with gold and jewels.

Zoom In

What detail tells when the soldier's account of his journey begins?

N
W   E
S

ATLANTIC OCEAN

Gulf of Mexico

CUBA

HISPANIOLA

◇ Tenochtitlán

YUCATÁN
PENINSULA

Caribbean Sea

Key

   Aztec Lands

– – – Route of Cortés

August 16, 1519

Today we met some of the Aztecs. They wear so much gold! So the stories are true, after all. Something even more amazing has happened. The Aztecs think Cortés is a god called Quetzalcoatl. They bow to him.

November 8, 1519

The journey to the Aztec city has been long. On the way, we met the Tlaxcalans, who are at war with the Aztecs. Cortés has a plan. Secretly, he makes a deal with the Tlaxcalans. We don't know how strong the Aztecs are. We need fighters on our side if there is a war.

November 25, 1519

The Aztec capital is amazing. Its name is
Tenochtitlán, and I think it must be the most beautiful
city in the world. The Aztecs still think that Cortés is a
god. He will use that to gain power over the Aztecs.
What an easy way to get rich!

Zoom In

Why does Cortés make a deal
with the Tlaxcalans?

July 1, 1520

We thought it would be easy to **conquer** the Aztecs. We have cannons, and they don't. We captured their **ruler**, Montezuma. We thought we were in power.

Then the Aztecs attacked. We tried to sneak out of the city, but the Aztecs heard us. They trapped us on the lake. Montezuma is dead. We lost many **soldiers** in the **conflict**. Our gold is mostly gone, too! Only a few of us got away.

April 28, 1521

Soon it will be our turn to attack. We have a whole army of Tlaxcalans. Cortés plans to take the city peacefully, but he is ready for war if it comes to that.

Prove It

How do the journal writer's feelings change throughout his journey? What evidence did you use for your answer?

August 13, 1521

We have been fighting for 75 days. Tenochtitlán is crumbling. The Aztec warriors are too weak to fight. Today, we captured their new ruler. The Aztec empire is ours! Cortés rules it now. He is to be called the Governor of New Spain.

January 15, 1524

A new city stands on the ruins of Tenochtitlán. Cortés will call it Mexico City. All of us in his army are rich now. Still, I am sorry that things ended this way. The beautiful Aztec city is gone. Many Aztecs have died. Is our glory worth all that?

Cortés and the End of the Aztec Empire

by Abigail Morris

The Spanish first arrived in what they called the "New World" in 1492. Over the years, more people from Spain came to the area. They were looking for gold.

In 1517, Spanish explorers made a couple of trips to the Yucatán Peninsula. They encountered the local people. They saw signs of an advanced civilization: buildings, art, gold jewelry, and other riches.

In 1519, Hernando Cortés was chosen to go back to the Yucatán territory to explore some more. Cortés was a conquistador. This is a Spanish word that means "conqueror." He got together a group of soldiers and ships. They set out to conquer the people and get their gold.

Cortés was not afraid of conflict. If any group would not do what he said, he attacked them. He killed many local people. He scared them with his horses and his weapons. These were both things the people had never seen before. News of his bloody tactics spread across the territory.

The Aztecs were the strongest group in the area. They lived in the Valley of Mexico and ruled over a large empire. But they treated the other tribes in the area badly and so were hated by everyone. This was a piece of good luck for Cortés. Many agreed to join with him in order to defeat the Aztecs.

Montezuma was the Aztecs' ruler. He heard reports of the Spanish conquistador. He thought that Cortés could be one of the Aztec gods returning to take back his kingdom.

Montezuma's belief was more good luck for Cortés. Even though Cortés had only a few men, he decided to travel to Tenochtitlán, the capital of the Aztec empire. There he would see for himself what riches he could take for Spain.

Cortés and his men entered the city on November 8, 1519. They thought they must be dreaming. Tenochtitlán was bigger and more beautiful than any Spanish city at the time. It had temples, palaces, a great market, houses, and gardens.

The city was built in the middle of a lake. Raised roads connected it to the mainland. It had streets and also canals. People could travel by canoe or on foot. Fresh water flowed into Tenochtitlán along specially built channels.

The people of Tenochtitlán grew crops on plots of land. These were areas of land in the lake, separated by canals. They were also called "floating gardens."

In Tenochtitlán, the Spanish were outnumbered. So they took Montezuma hostage and demanded gold for his return. They melted down the Aztecs' treasure and sent the gold to Spain. It seemed as if Cortés and his men had won a war without any fighting.

Later, when Cortés was away from the city, the soldiers he had left behind in Tenochtitlán killed many Aztec leaders. Montezuma died as well. The Aztecs fought back, killing many Spanish.

Cortés could not go back into the city. He retreated over the mountains to rebuild his army and plan an attack on Tenochtitlán. He got help from the local people who wanted to break away from Aztec rule.

The Aztecs were regrouping as well. But then, many began to die from smallpox. This was a new illness **introduced** by the Spanish. The remaining Aztecs were weak and disorganized.

In a few short months, Cortés was able to crush the Aztecs and their empire. Soon the Spaniards would begin building a new city, Mexico City, on the ruins of Tenochtitlán.

Prove It

Use details from the selection to describe the Aztec city of Tenochtitlán.

THE EARLIEST AMERICANS

by Osvaldo Alvarez

▲ Mayan city of Palenque

There were many **Native American** civilizations in North, Central, and South America long before any Europeans arrived. Three important ones were the Maya, the Inca, and the Aztec. These cultures were rich in art, religion, and learning. Their people built great cities out of stone. They did complex mathematics. They studied the skies and kept calendars. Spanish conquistadors conquered the Aztecs and the Inca. The Mayan civilization died out on its own hundreds of years before the Spanish arrived.

Civilizations of the Early Americas

The Mayan Mystery

The Maya settled on the Yucatán Peninsula over 3,000 years ago. They lived in small villages and farmed the land. Over time, the villages grew and became large cities.

At the height of Mayan civilization, there were more than 40 cities. The cities had huge stone buildings, including palaces, pyramids, and temples. Between 5,000 and 50,000 people lived in each city.

The Mayans probably never had an empire. Mayan cities shared the same culture and **customs**, but each had its own king. There was trade between the cities. Sometimes wars broke out.

The Mayan civilization was advanced. They created one of the first writing systems in the Americas. They knew astronomy and mathematics.

By around A.D. 900, the Maya had left their cities. Their civilization fell apart. No one knows exactly why.

Zoom In

What information does the timeline give about the Mayan civilization?

▼ Mayan ruins at Tulum

2000 | Maya live on the Yucatán Peninsula.

900 | Maya leave cities.

2000 | 1000 | **B.C.** ◆ **A.D.** 1000 |

The Aztecs' City on a Lake

The Aztecs seem to have arrived in the Valley of Mexico in A.D. 1345. They were the last group to move into the area. So they had to take swampy land that no one else wanted. The Aztecs went to work and made something wonderful. Over the years they "reclaimed" land from the swamp by adding dirt and building up the ground. Little by little they built a beautiful city, Tenochtitlán.

At the center of the city were temples and other public buildings. Many were painted in bright colors. The temples were important since religion played a big part in everyday life for the Aztecs. Their religious customs included worshipping many gods.

The palaces of the rulers were also at the center of the city. The palaces had their own gardens and zoos. Aztec rulers were treated almost like gods.

▲ Aztec artifacts

1345 | Aztecs settle in what is now Mexico City.

When the Aztecs first arrived in the area, they were ruled over by more powerful local tribes. But soon they joined with others and fought. In 1428 they defeated the tribes ruling over them. Now they started to conquer other tribes in the area. Over time their city on the lake became the capital of a powerful empire.

The Aztec Empire came to an end in 1521. That was the year Cortés's soldiers destroyed Tenochtitlán. When the Aztec's main city was destroyed, the empire collapsed.

▼ Aztec ruins in Mexico City

The Inca and Their Road System

The Inca lived in cities high in the Andes Mountains of Peru. Their main city was called Cusco. The first Inca ruler moved his tribe to Cusco sometime in the twelfth century. At first, the Inca lived in peace with their neighbors.

In the fourteenth century, the Inca began to expand their territory. They conquered other tribes. They kept tight control over the areas they conquered in two ways. First, Inca soldiers went to live in the newly captured areas. They kept an eye on the people. Second, the Inca moved some of the captured people to faraway places. This made it hard for anyone to organize and fight back.

At its height, the Inca Empire stretched more than 2,000 miles along the west coast of South America. It was centered in the Andes Mountains. But it also included dry coastal areas and tropical rain forests.

1531– Hernando de Soto and Francisco
1533 Pizarro conquer the Incan Empire.

1530

1540

The empire was connected from one end to the other with good roads and strong rope bridges. A system of relay runners carried messages quickly from place to place. For example, runners made the 1,250-mile journey between the cities of Quito and Cusco in just five days.

The Inca were amazing builders. They built cities of stone high up in the mountains. Religion was important to the Inca. Priests honored Incan **ancestors** and the gods.

In the 1500s, Spanish conquistadors arrived. Hernando de Soto and Francisco Pizarro traveled to Cusco. They defeated the Inca empire.

New Foods, New Ideas

The Native Americans introduced the Spanish explorers to new customs and to foods such as sugar, potatoes, and corn.

Prove It

Which of these empires encountered the Spanish conquistadors? How do you know?

1550 Spanish settlements spread across the Americas.

Learn the Words

capital
ruler
empire
conquistador
introduce
encounter
conflict
conquer

- Read the words on the list.
- Read the dialogue.
- Find the words.

These ruins were the ancient **capital** of a great **empire**.

How did the empire fall? Did a **conquistador** and his army **conquer** it?

1. What's Your Version?
Listening and Speaking

Think about how the people in the picture found these ruins. Tell your partner what most likely happened. Then listen to your partner tell the same story. How is each person's version alike? How is it different?

2. Make a Venn Diagram
Graphic Organizer

Work with a partner. Think about the Mayan number system. Think about our number system. What is true about just one of the number systems? What is true about both number systems? Show your findings on a Venn diagram.

Mayan number system — both — Our number system

3. You Are the Reporter
Writing

Suppose you could travel in time. You can visit the Aztec, the Inca, or the Maya. What would you ask the people? Write five questions you would ask about their lives. Share your questions with your partner.

4. Make a Drawing
Speaking and Listening

Design a capital city. It can be in the past or the present. Show at least five buildings. Tell your partner about the buildings.

Horses on the Plains

by Richard Begay

Horses were introduced to the Americas by the Spanish. In fact, it would be better to say they were re-introduced. Long ago, wild horses roamed across the plains of North America. These were the ancestors of modern horses. They died out about 11,000 years ago.

When Cortés and the other conquistadors came to North, Central, and South America, they brought horses with them. Some of these horses escaped. They bred and multiplied and formed wild herds. The Spanish also traded horses with native tribes. In these two ways, horses began to spread up into the Great Plains of North America.

Horses changed the lives and cultures of many Native American tribes living on the Great Plains. Because of the horse, some tribes changed their whole way of life in just a few years.

Before horses, dogs were the only tamed animals on the plains. Dogs could not carry a lot. This made it difficult for people to move with their belongings from place to place. So they tended to stay put.

Horses could carry heavier loads than dogs could. This made it easier for people to move around. Groups began to travel from place to place.

Horses could also carry people. It was easier to hunt buffalo on horseback than on foot. Buffalo became the main food source for some groups. They would pack up everything and move across the plains, following the buffalo herds.

Moving about over longer distances meant that more groups came into contact with each other. Sometimes that contact led to conflict. But for the most part, the introduction of horses was a huge improvement for the people of the Great Plains.

The Mysterious Mound Builders

by Vera Simmons

▲ Drawing of how Monk's Mound might have looked around 1850

Not many people today have heard of Cahokia. But this bustling Native American city has an important place in history. Cahokia seems to have been the first city in North America. Cahokia thrived and then disappeared. It was long gone by the time European explorers arrived.

The area around Cahokia, in what is now Illinois, was settled by about A.D. 700. By 1200, at least 15,000 people lived there. The people of Cahokia caught fish on the Mississippi River. They grew corn in fields nearby. They also built large mounds of mud. They built houses and temples on top of the mounds.

Monk's Mound had a surface as big as ten football fields. It was 100 feet tall. That's ten stories high. It is the largest mound in North America. To build it, the people of Cahokia had to carry heavy baskets of dirt on their backs. They had to make millions and millions of trips. They kept building the mound up higher and higher over about 300 years.

A City Vanishes

Cahokia grew quickly, and it died quickly. By about 1250, Cahokia was beginning to fall apart. Its good soil had disappeared. Its rivers had flooded over. Its people had cut down many trees from nearby forests for houses, forts, walls, and firewood. The people of Cahokia made a wall around the inner city, probably for protection. They used 20,000 trees to build the wall. Then they rebuilt the wall three more times.

When crops did not grow, many people starved. This led to wars with neighboring peoples and other problems. People began moving away. By 1400, Cahokia had been left behind.

▼ **Archaeologist working at Cahokia**

Prove It
What details in the text give reasons that people may have moved away from Cahokia?

Retell "Sailing with Cortés"

> ℹ️ When you retell a story, you tell only the most important events. Tell the events in order. You can use dates in your retelling. Using words such as *first, next, then,* and *finally* will also help listeners understand the order of events.

"Sailing with Cortés" is a diary, or journal. Each event begins with the date when it took place. Review the selection on pages 210–215. Look at the pictures on page 233.

■ First Picture: What important events happened on March 25, 1519?

■ Second Picture: What events does the journal tell about on this date?

■ Third and Fourth Pictures: What events does the journal tell about on those dates?

Use the pictures on page 233 to retell the selection to your partner. As you retell each event, point to the correct picture. Use complete sentences.

Words you might use in your retelling:		
soldier	ruler	empire
conquer	ruins	conquistador

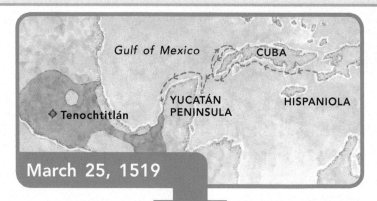

Gulf of Mexico

CUBA

YUCATÁN PENINSULA

HISPANIOLA

◇ Tenochtitlán

March 25, 1519

November 25, 1519

July 1, 1520

January 15, 1524

Dig Deeper

Look Back

Compare the selections "Sailing with Cortés" and "Cortés and the End of the Aztec Empire." On a sheet of paper, answer these questions.

1. In which selection does a person tell about an event he saw with his own eyes?

2. Which selection gives more information about what Montezuma did?

3. What fact about Mexico City is in both selections?

Talk About It

How can we combine two sentences?

The Maya built amazing cities.
By around the year 900, they had left their cities.

The Maya built amazing cities, but by around the year 900, they had left their cities.

Now it's your turn. Work with a partner. Come up with two sentences that can be combined with *but*.

Conversation

 You can talk about your hopes and wishes. A hope is something that you believe can happen someday. A wish might or might not happen.

Talk to a partner. One of you will be person A. The other will be person B.

Person A

Person A

Ask what your partner hopes for.

Reply. Ask what wish your partner has.

Thank your partner.

Person B

Person B

Reply. Ask what your partner hopes for.

Reply. Ask what your partner's wish is.

Say goodbye to your partner.

UNDER THE CANOPY

The **BIG** Question

How do plants and animals depend on each other?

☐ What is life like in a rain forest?

☐ How do animals live in the rain forest? What kinds of plants can live in a rain forest?

☐ Why is it important to protect Earth's rain forests?

Why are rain forests an unusual ecosystem?

1. **How are rain forests different from other forests?**

   Rain forests have...

   ☐ much more rainfall!

   ☐ more plants and trees.

   ☐ lots of moss.

   ☐ lots of vines.

vines

2. **How do plants adapt to rain forest life?**

   Some plants...

   ☐ have roots that don't need soil.

   ☐ have long, hollow stems.

   ☐ can grow on other plants.

plants on tree

3. How do animals in the rain
   forest move around?

   Some animals…

   ☐ climb trees.

   ☐ swing by their tails.

   ☐ hop.

   ☐ fly.

4. Why must we protect rain forests?

   Rain forests…

   ☐ have many different plants and animals.

   ☐ have plants that make good medicines.

   ☐ are a home for many people and animals.

Say **more!**

Learn the Words

ecosystem
adaptation
tropical
humid
forest floor
understory
canopy
emergent layer

Theme Vocabulary

The easiest way to remember the meaning of a new word is to use the word. As you discuss rain forests, use these vocabulary words. Use them when you read and write about rain forests, too.

Read the word.
Look at the picture.
Listen to your teacher.

ecosystem

adaptation

tropical

humid

forest floor

understory

canopy

emergent layer

How Do You Feel?

Look at the vocabulary cards. Choose one picture and tell how
it makes you feel.

Beware of the Slime

Panel 1

Ramita: Hey, Greg. What do you have there?

Keep It Green

Greg: It's my science report.

Panel 2

Ramita: "Green Slime"?

Greg: Yep. Want to check it out?

Ramita: Sure.

GREEN SLIME

Panel 3

GREEN SLIME

by: Greg Clay.

Panel 4

Green Slime is all over the place. You can't always see it, but it's here.

Panel 5

Green Slime hides in shrubs and grass. If you step on it, it will grab you. It will suck you in.

Panel 6

Green Slime hangs from trees till you go by.

 14 Formal/Informal Language When you "give someone a heads-up," you warn the person about something. Would it be more acceptable to say this to a friend or a teacher? Explain.

19 What are you doing?

I want to see what it does.

20 Why isn't it moving?

Who cares? We have to get out while we can!

21 Are you crazy?

Something doesn't add up here.

22 Hmmm...This feels a lot like gelatin.

23 Lime gelatin, to be exact.

24 Nice try, Greg.

> **21 Formal/Informal Language** Saying that "something doesn't add up" is an informal way to say "something doesn't make sense."

245

Rain Forests of

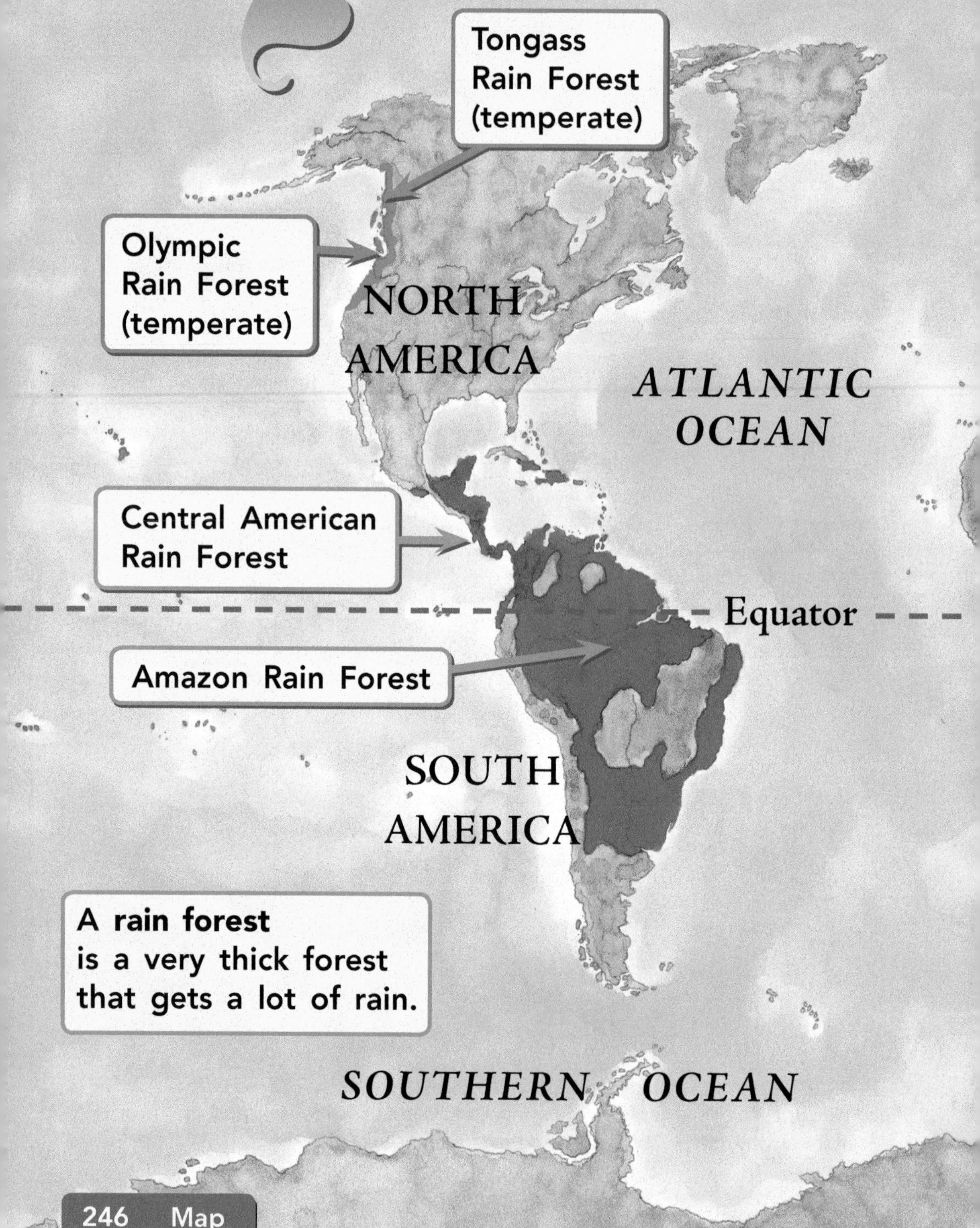

Tongass
Rain Forest
(temperate)

Olympic
Rain Forest
(temperate)

NORTH
AMERICA

ATLANTIC
OCEAN

Central American
Rain Forest

Equator

Amazon Rain Forest

SOUTH
AMERICA

A rain forest
is a very thick forest
that gets a lot of rain.

SOUTHERN OCEAN

the World

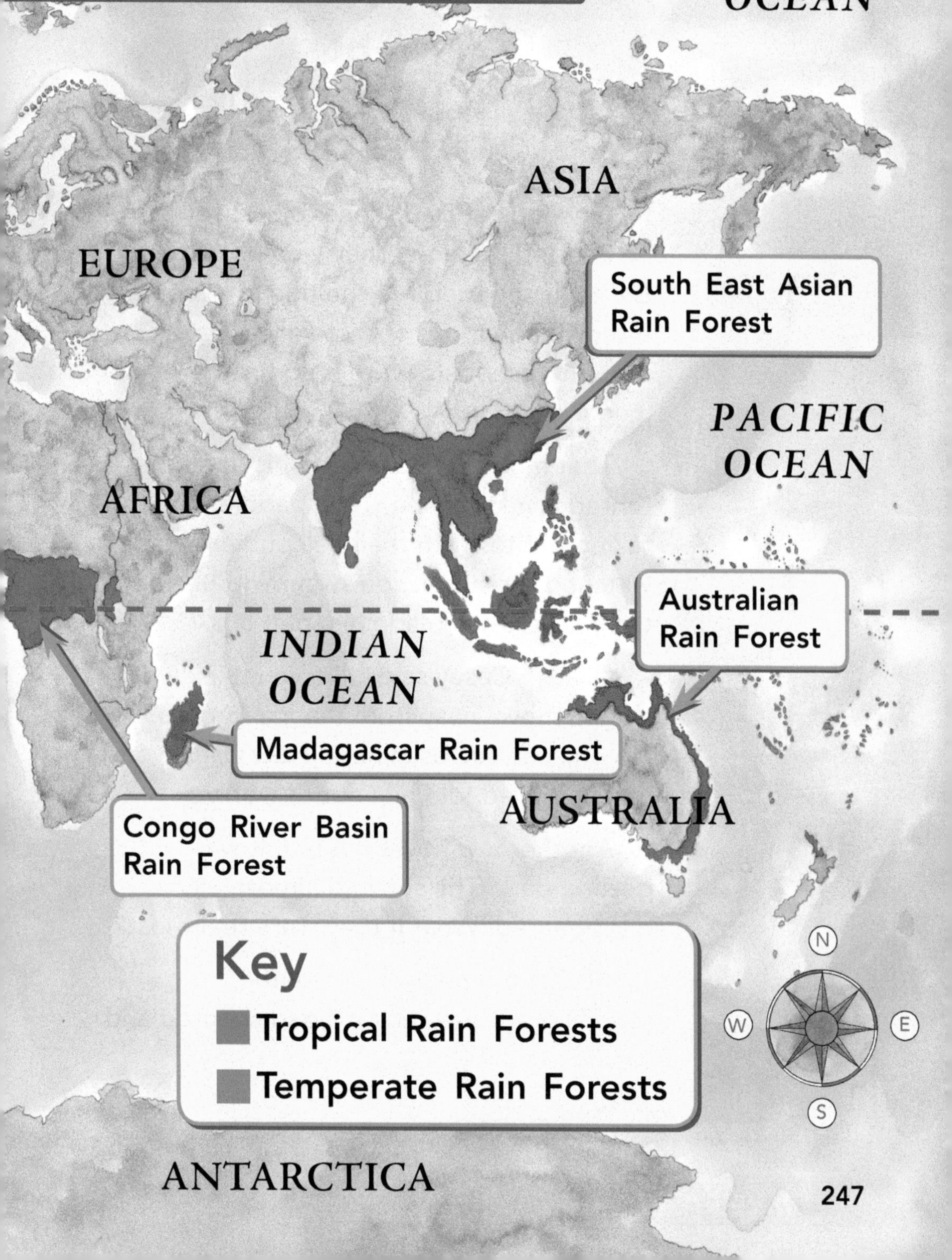

ARCTIC
OCEAN

ASIA

EUROPE

South East Asian
Rain Forest

PACIFIC
OCEAN

AFRICA

Australian
Rain Forest

INDIAN
OCEAN

Madagascar Rain Forest

Congo River Basin
Rain Forest

AUSTRALIA

Key
Tropical Rain Forests
Temperate Rain Forests

N

W · E

S

ANTARCTICA

Lost in Belize
by Dylan Gold

One look at Dad's face told Casey all he needed to know. They were lost. *Lost in Belize!* It sounded like the title of a story. If they made it out of there alive, Casey thought, he would write it up for the school magazine.

That morning, Casey and his dad had rented a small canoe. They paddled around taking photos with their cell phones. Casey watched the barracuda swimming beside the canoe. They made him nervous.

"Dad?" Casey said. "Do you think we should move away from the mangroves? No one can see us in here. How will anyone find us?" Dad told him not to worry.

Another few hours passed. It was getting dark. The sun had almost disappeared. What if they were really lost?

At that moment, they saw the searchlight. Casey and his dad shouted and waved.

But wait! The light was moving away from them! Then Casey remembered something.

"I have a flashlight on my cell," he said. "It's small, but it's bright."

Casey turned on his cell and pressed the flashlight app. He shouted as the bright light shone on the water. Slowly, the search boat turned toward them.

By the time Casey and Dad were safely on board the skiff, everyone was laughing—especially the rescue workers.

One of the workers kept staring at one of Casey's photos and asked him to enlarge it. The smudge of yellow in the trees turned out to be a bird. But not just any bird! It was a yellow spotted humplesnapper, which was thought to be extinct. In time, Casey's photo would become famous in the birder community.

Rain Forest Plants

Tropical rain forests are hot, wet, and steamy. They are an **ecosystem** with tons of **diversity**. There are more kinds of plants in a rain forest than anywhere else on Earth.

It is important to try to **preserve** the rain forest. Rain forest plants are used to make medicine. In fact, about one-fourth of all medicines come from tropical rain forest plants.

Trees in a tropical rain forest grow so thick that they block sunlight. Plants have developed **adaptations** to get the sun they need. Here are some amazing rain forest plants.

← 7 feet →

flower

Amazon water lily

The Amazon water lily lives in lakes and flooded areas. It has huge flowers and leaves. Sharp spines on the bottom of the leaves **protect** them from fish and other animals. Its stems lie buried in mud below the water.

bamboo

Bamboo grows on the **forest floor**. It has long, hollow stems. It grows quickly to try to reach the sunlight. Bamboo reaches up to 100 feet tall. People can use bamboo to make almost anything, such as flutes, fishing poles, furniture, and even houses.

bird of paradise

The bird of paradise plant has colorful flowers that look like bird's heads. Its leaves can be more than two feet long. The stems of the flowers can be five feet long.

bougainvillea

Bougainvillea has leaves shaped like little hearts. The flowers can be purple, pink, red, orange, white, or yellow. Bougainvillea can grow as a vine, tree, or shrub. It can grow in full sun or in the shade. It has thorns to protect it from being eaten.

liana

A liana is a vine. It starts from the ground and then climbs or twines around other plants. It climbs until it reaches the sunlight at the forest canopy. At the top, it can spread to other trees, tangling them together. Monkeys and apes climb on the long stems.

orchid

An orchid has flowers with beautiful colors. Orchids in tropical rain forests grow high up on trees. They don't have roots in the ground. They get water from the air. There are as many as 25,000 different types of orchids.

pitcher plant

A pitcher plant is one of the few plants that eats animals. It is shaped like a pitcher. It attracts its **prey** with bright colors and sweet smells. Insects, and sometimes even small mice or lizards, go into the pitcher and get trapped. Pitcher plants can grow on the forest floor or in the canopy.

rafflesia

Rafflesia has huge flowers. In fact, they are the biggest flowers in the world. It has no roots or leaves. Rafflesia grows inside the vines or trunks of another plant, taking its water and food. It is seen only when the huge flower comes out and begins to bloom.

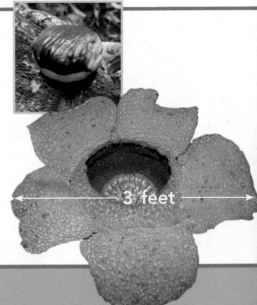

3 feet

red ginger

The red flowering ginger plant has wide leaves. It grows in stalks. A bright red flower grows out of the top of the stalk.

Spanish moss

Spanish moss grows high up on trees. It has long silver-green stems. Clumps of Spanish moss on branches look like beards or fur. It gets water and nutrients from the rain and the air.

strangler fig

A strangler fig starts as a plant that grows on another tree. Monkeys and birds leave the small, sticky seeds high up in the branches. The young strangler figs live up in the canopy, getting water from the humid air. Then they grow long roots and send them down to the ground. The roots grow quickly. They often choke and kill host trees.

Prove It

What do rain forest plants have to adapt to? How do you know?

The Wettest Place on Earth

by Patricia Almada

The rain forest,
The wettest place on Earth,
Is painted a bright palette
Of every shade of green.
Towering trees look down
On the scurrying insects below.
Climbing plants and strangling vines
Inch up trunks and branches,
Hoping to reach the golden prize
That shines beyond the canopy.

Air plants,
Needing only water and air,
Live on trees like uninvited guests.
Their leaves form buckets—
Watery pools where salamanders swim.
The rain forest,
The wettest place on Earth,
Splashes the world with its many gifts.

Hiking
in a Cloud Forest

by Katacha Díaz

The Monteverde Cloud Forest Preserve is in Costa Rica. It is the world's best-known tropical cloud forest. A cloud forest is a wet ecosystem high in the mountains. Clouds and fog cover the forest canopy. The water drips down onto the leaves below.

A cloud forest has many plants that get their water and nutrients from the air and rain. They live perched on other plants, sometimes high up off the ground.

Monteverde is dense and green. A wide diversity of plants live in the different layers of the forest. The rain forest **provides** a home to many animals as well. Cloud forest animals have made adaptations to their special environment. Some of these animals can't be found anywhere else in the world.

March 1   1:00 P.M.

We have just arrived in the rain forest. It is so green! But it is darker than I expected. Maybe that is because of all the clouds and fog hanging over everything. It is so wet, I can't believe it isn't raining.

We don't see any of the tropical animals yet. But we know they are there. Many of them are well **camouflaged**. We think we are looking at a leaf or branch, but really it is an animal. The animal has adapted to be hidden in plain sight. We can't see them, but all around, hidden eyes are watching us!

cloud forest

Zoom In

What does the author mean when she says that hidden eyes are watching? Where did you find your answer?

Forest Floor

The forest floor is shady. Very little sunlight reaches there. Because of this, very few plants grow all the way down on the forest floor. The few plants that do grow on the forest floor are specially adapted to need little light.

The forest floor is covered with wet leaves, fallen branches, seeds, and fruit. Because it is so wet and dark, everything on the forest floor rots very quickly. Trees' shallow roots grow on the surface of the forest floor. That's because the soil in the tropical cloud forest is not very deep.

Lots of insects and spiders live on the forest floor. Large animals such as tapirs, deer, and jaguars live there, too.

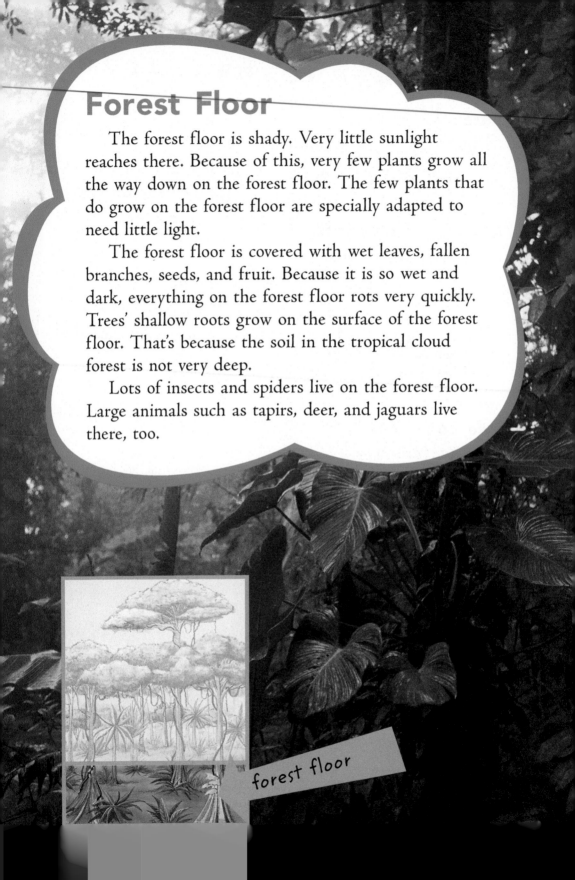

forest floor

March 1

3:00 P.M.

I picked up a long, green twig from the forest floor. It moved! That really surprised me. It was a walkingstick, an insect that looks like a stick. The camouflage helps protect it. The walkingstick is part of a **food chain** of **predators** and prey. It doesn't want to get eaten!

Walkingsticks stay still during the day. Maybe that's why I thought it was just a stick. At night they search for leaves. Other insects, like leafcutter ants, eat leaves from the forest floor as well.

walkingstick

Understory

The **understory** is the area of the rain forest between the canopy and the forest floor. It is shady, cool, and humid. It does not get very much of the sunlight that falls onto the forest. It is where ferns, bushes, and smaller trees grow.

Plants in the understory often have large leaves so they can catch as much sunlight as possible. Compared to the rain forest's canopy, the understory is quite open. Woody vines grow around tree trunks and climb toward the sunlight.

There are lots of insects in the understory. There are also snakes, frogs, lizards, small mammals, and birds. Most of the birds live on or in tree bark or make their nests in little hollows in the trees. Jaguars crouch on branches in the understory, looking for prey. A jaguar is a predator. It is at the very top of the food chain.

understory

March 2   9:00 A.M.

Our teacher told us to sit quietly, look, and listen. After a while, we started to notice all the life around us. We could see so many animals in the understory! Here's some of what we saw:

• Red-eyed tree frog: it was stuck to the bottom of a leaf, asleep. Someone jiggled the branch by mistake. The frog woke up. It flashed its red eyes and orange feet and jumped away.

• Clearwing butterfly: I looked through its wings and saw a flower on the other side.

• Blue-crowned motmot: This bird had a bright blue cap. It had feather tassels at the end of its tail that twitched back and forth.

blue-crowned motmot

Zoom In

What are some animals that live in the understory? Where did you find your answer?

261

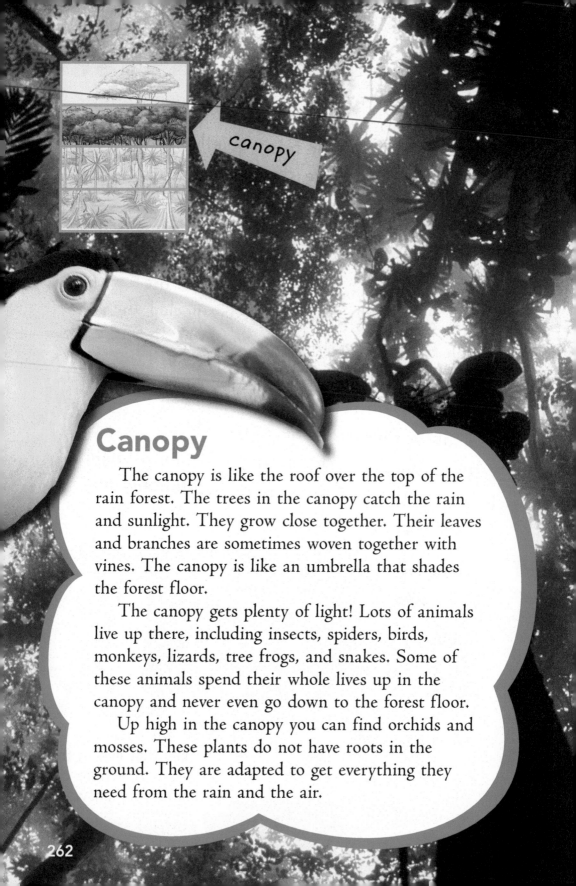

canopy

Canopy

The canopy is like the roof over the top of the rain forest. The trees in the canopy catch the rain and sunlight. They grow close together. Their leaves and branches are sometimes woven together with vines. The canopy is like an umbrella that shades the forest floor.

The canopy gets plenty of light! Lots of animals live up there, including insects, spiders, birds, monkeys, lizards, tree frogs, and snakes. Some of these animals spend their whole lives up in the canopy and never even go down to the forest floor.

Up high in the canopy you can find orchids and mosses. These plants do not have roots in the ground. They are adapted to get everything they need from the rain and the air.

March 2   12:00 P.M.

The forest canopy is so dense that I can't see the sky. I stand inside a huge, hollow strangler fig and look up. It's like a long, dark tunnel. I use my binoculars and see spotted flowers. They are air plants growing high up on a tree.

Suddenly I hear a lot of loud noises. I look up again. There are six toucans high up in the canopy. I can tell they are toucans because they have huge yellow bills. They look almost like bananas! They call out to each other. I guess they are not afraid of being heard.

strangler fig

Emergent Layer

The tallest trees in the rain forest reach above the canopy. They form the **emergent layer**. That is the highest layer of the forest. Emergent trees can grow several hundred feet tall. Their tops are shaped a bit like mushrooms. They tower over the rest of the forest.

Trees in the emergent layer are spaced out farther from each other than those in the canopy. These trees get the most sunlight. But they also have to be able to stand up to high temperatures, less water, and strong winds.

Eagles and other birds, monkeys, bats, and butterflies are some of the animals that live in the emergent layer of the rain forest.

emergent trees

emergent layer

3:00 P.M.

March 2

As we leave in a helicopter, we look out over the very top of the rain forest. I can see an eagle perched at the top of a tall tree. I think I can see some beautiful orchids blooming above the canopy. I guess a helicopter is a pretty good way to see the top of the forest!

The cloud forest is a magical place. It is full of hidden treasures! We saw a lot, but there is much, much more to see. I hope I can come back and visit again soon.

orchids

Prove It

What details show how the emergent layer is different from the forest floor?

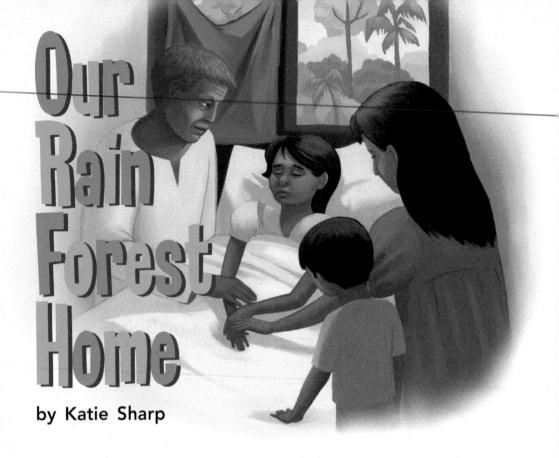

Our Rain Forest Home

by Katie Sharp

This morning my sister, Esmerelda, woke up feeling sick. Mother went in. She felt her head and listened to her breathing.

"She needs medicine," said Mother. "Miguel, go tell your grandfather."

When we're sick, Grandfather makes medicine from the rain forest plants near our home. He knows exactly which ones to use for every purpose.

"Come, Miguel," he said when I told him about Esmerelda. "Help me gather the plants I need."

I walked with Grandfather towards the forest. I noticed many trees had been cut down. Grandfather started to look worried.

"What's wrong?" I asked.

"Miguel," he replied, "the plants I need are becoming scarce. We must walk farther to find the liana."

"Why is this happening?" I asked.

"People want to make room for banana plantations and cattle ranches," Grandfather explained. "They come and cut down the trees. Our forests are destroyed. They don't understand."

Zoom In

What is the problem in the story? How can you find out?

"What don't they understand, Grandfather?" I asked,
feeling very small and sad.

"They don't understand that trees of the rain forest provide
food and a place to live. Without those trees, many plants and
animals are dying. Soon even our way of life may disappear."

Finally, Grandfather spotted a liana twisted around a tree.
I helped pull it free, and Grandfather cut it. We were careful
not to destroy the whole plant. We took just what we needed
and left the rest so the liana could continue to grow.

As we returned home, Grandfather said, "There is some good news, Miguel. In some places, the forest is growing back. People around the world are starting to help protect the rain forest. It will be up to you and all Bribri children to make sure the rain forest survives. That is the only way our way of life will survive."

Right then, I made a promise to always help protect the forest and my people.

Prove It

What promise did Miguel make? How do you know?

269

The Hedge and the

Characters

ALBERT: a young man   ALICE: his sister

Scene 1

Setting: A grape vineyard near a main road. ALBERT stands near the field with ALICE.

ALBERT: I'm glad Father left the vineyards to me. I'm going to make some changes around here.

ALICE: Really? Why? What kind of changes?

ALBERT: First of all, I'm going to get rid of these hedges. They are useless! They don't grow any grapes. They just take up space.

ALICE: But the hedges are beautiful! They give shade, and birds make their nests in them. The hedges protect the field. Father always said they were important.

ALBERT: I don't care about protecting the fields! What's important is that I own them, and I can do what I like. Father was old-fashioned. He didn't know how to make money from the farm. Just wait and see.

Vineyard

a play adapted from a fable by Aesop

Scene 2

Setting: The same vineyard, but the grapes on the vines are all gone. ALBERT stands in the empty field with his sister.

ALBERT: What happened? All the grapes are gone! Who did this? What fool has destroyed my crop? No one ever stole grapes from this field before!

ALICE: No one stole before because the field was protected. Behind the hedge, the travelers walking down the road could not see the tasty grapes. You took down the hedge, and see what happened?

ALBERT: *(hanging his head)* You are right. The fool who destroyed the crop is me. I'm sorry. I didn't know the hedge was so important. I guess I've learned a lesson.

ALICE: Yes. And that lesson is...?

ALBERT: It is just as important to protect what you have as it is to own it.

Prove It

Why did Albert want to get rid of the hedges? Where did you find your answer?

Learn the Words

preserve
protect
provide
diversity
food chain
predator
prey
camouflage

- Read the words on the list.
- Read the dialogue.
- Find the words.

The lake and trees **provide** shelter for many animals.

This forest has great **diversity**.

We must **preserve** and **protect** this place.

1. Make a Venn Diagram
Graphic Organizer

What can you see in a forest like the one in the picture? What can you see in a city? What can you see in both places? Make a Venn diagram. Show it to your partner.

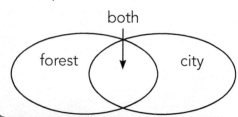

both

forest   city

2. Make a Drawing
Listening and Speaking

Many animals have skin or fur patterns that help them hide from predators. Draw a real or made-up animal. Its coat should have a pattern that camouflages it. Share your picture with a partner.

3. Make a Speech
Listening and Speaking

What things in nature do you most want to protect and preserve? Write a short speech about your topic. Work on your speech with your partner. Be sure to give your opinions in the speech. Give your speech to the class.

4. Write a Journal Entry
Writing

Pretend that you visit a rain forest. What do you see? How do you feel about your trip? Write a journal entry. Tell about your visit. You can use the journal entries in "Hiking in a Cloud Forest" in this unit as a model. Show your letter to your partner.

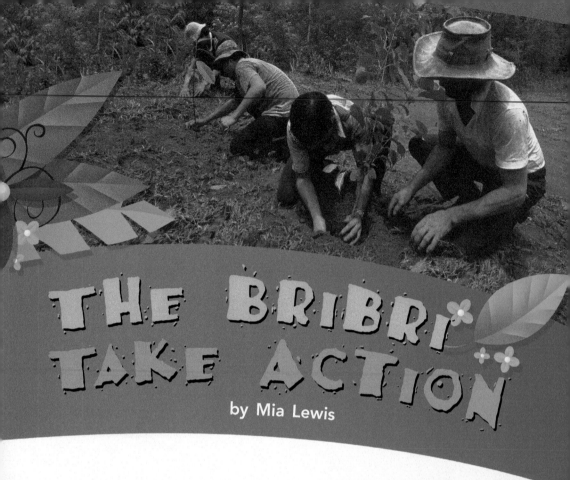

THE BRIBRI TAKE ACTION

by Mia Lewis

The Bribri are a Native American tribe. They have lived in the rain forests of Costa Rica for thousands of years. They lived there before the Spanish first arrived, in 1502. Some of them still live there today. They speak the Bribri language. They live by their own customs.

The Bribri are farmers. Inside the rain forest, they grow more than 120 different types of plants. They use the plants for food, medicine, building and craft materials, and firewood, and to sell or trade. The way they farm does not hurt the soil or the forest. It does not pollute the water. It does not threaten the insects, birds, or animals of the forest.

The Bribri also harvest food, medicine, and materials from the forest. They know how to get what they need from the forest without harming it.

The Bribri live in harmony with the natural world. Even though they are farmers, they depend on the rain forest. They cannot continue their way of life without the forest. But every year, thousands of acres of rain forest in Costa Rica are destroyed.

The Bribri are losing their natural habitat, so they are buying back land and replanting it with native plants and trees. The Bribri are working hard to preserve their way of life in the rain forests of Costa Rica.

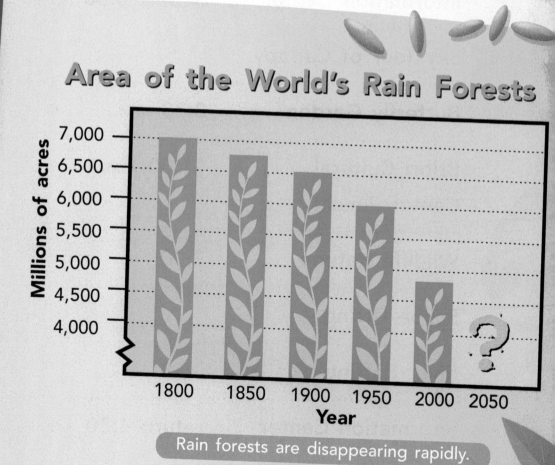

Area of the World's Rain Forests

Rain forests are disappearing rapidly.

Costa Rican
RAIN FOREST TOURS

Family

Information Center	depart 8:00 A.M.
Sky Tour of Canopy	
Butterfly Garden	8:30 A.M.
Bribri Cultural Center (lunch)	11:00 A.M.
Wildlife Refuge	2:00 P.M.
Scuba Diving	
River Rafting	
Information Center	return 4:30 P.M.

Adventure	Nature Lovers
depart 9:00 A.M.	depart 9:30 A.M.
9:30 A.M.	
	10:00 A.M.
12:30 P.M.	12:00 P.M.
	1:30 P.M.
2:00 P.M.	3:30 P.M.
4:30 P.M.	
return 7:00 P.M.	return 6:30 P.M.

Retell "Hiking in a Cloud Forest"

> (i) When you retell a selection, you give only the most important ideas and details. This helps listeners understand what the selection is mostly about. Use words like *for example*, *such as*, and *for instance* in your retelling.

Review the selection on pages 256–265. Look at the pictures on the timeline on page 279.

■ First Picture: What are the first details given about the forest?

■ Second and Third Pictures: What details are given about the forest floor and the understory?

■ Fourth and Fifth Pictures: What important details are given about the canopy and the emergent layer?

Use the timeline and the pictures on page 279 to retell the selection to your partner. As you give each important detail, point to the correct picture. Use complete sentences.

Words you might use in your retelling:		
tropical	humid	diversity
forest floor	understory	canopy

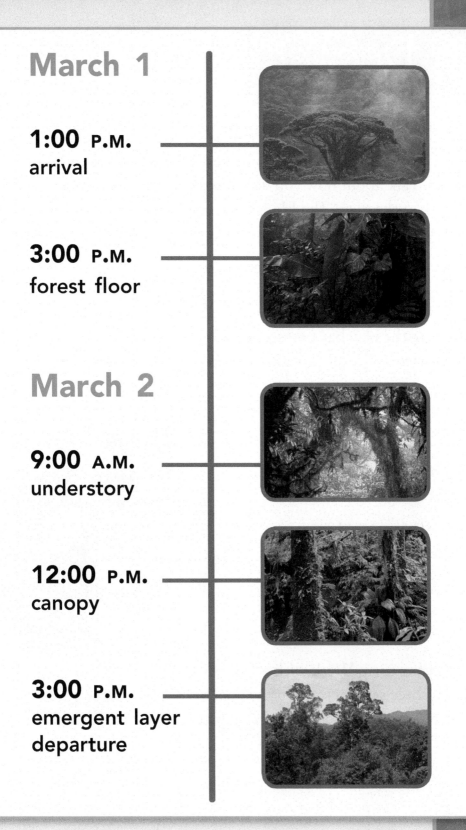

March 1

1:00 P.M.
arrival

3:00 P.M.
forest floor

March 2

9:00 A.M.
understory

12:00 P.M.
canopy

3:00 P.M.
emergent layer
departure

Dig Deeper

Look Back

Look back at the story "Our Rain Forest Home." Work with a partner. Talk about how you would make this story into a play. Look at the play "The Hedge and the Vineyard" for ideas. Work together to answer these questions.

1. Who would be in the cast of characters?

2. What settings would you describe for the play?

3. Suppose the play has two scenes. Where would Scene 2 begin? Why?

Each partner should write the answers on a sheet of paper.

Talk About It

Miguel tells **his** grandfather that Esmerelda is sick.

Grandfather uses **his** medicines to help people.

In each sentence above, what person's name could substitute for *his*? Is it the same person's name?

Now it's your turn. Work with a partner. Make up three sentences about Miguel or his grandfather. Use *he, him,* or *his* in each sentence. Have your partner see whether you used the words correctly.

Conversation

 To speak formally, use polite words. Speak carefully and don't use slang. You might show less feeling than normal.

Talk to a partner. One of you will be person A. The other will be person B.

Person A

Person B

Use **formal** language. Tell your partner about an event.

Reply in formal language. Ask how your partner feels about the event.

Reply in formal language.

Use **informal** language. Tell about the same event.

Reply in informal language. Ask how your partner feels about the event.

Reply in informal language.

Golden Opportunities

The **BIG** Question

How can businesses and customers help each other?

☐ Is it possible for children to start a business?

☐ What kind of plan should people make before starting a business?

☐ What are some ways to advertise a business?

What makes a business succeed?

1. What are some helpful business skills?

A business owner must…

- ☐ keep track of supplies.
- ☐ do math carefully.
- ☐ enjoy hard work.
- ☐ bring in customers.

2. What everyday activities can be turned into a business?

People can make a business out of…

- ☐ cooking.
- ☐ cleaning.
- ☐ organizing.
- ☐ caring for pets.

3. How do businesses help people?

Businesses can…

- ☐ provide a service that people need.
- ☐ sell things that people can't get themselves.
- ☐ make a neighborhood lively.
- ☐ let people shop from home.

4. How are all businesses alike?

In every business, the owner needs to…

- ☐ spend carefully.
- ☐ plan well.
- ☐ do a lot of work.
- ☐ give customers something they want or need.

Say more!

Learn the Words

business
profit
risk
hire
advertise
entrepreneur
customer
earn

Theme Vocabulary

 The easiest way to remember the meaning of a new word is to use the word. As you discuss businesses, use these vocabulary words. Use them when you read and write about businesses, too.

Read the word.
Look at the picture.
Listen to your teacher.

business

$50.00 Money earned at car wash
-$15.00 Supplies for car wash
$35.00 Profit

profit

risk

hire

advertise

entrepreneur

customer

earn

Match the Pictures

Look at the vocabulary cards. Choose two pictures that go together. Tell why you think the pictures go together.

Too Many Rules!

Sitha   Mr. Smith

1. SMITH'S MARKET — JUNE 21 — cat food

So, you say you want a job.

2. That's right, Mr. Smith. I'm ready to work.

3. Okay, Sitha, but this job is no picnic.

4. You have to work hard. And the most important thing is to follow the rules.

5

Let's see if you can stack these boxes correctly.

6

Make sure you follow all the rules. Understand?

Yes, sir.

7

8

1. If a box has a red spot on it, then you cannot stack it on a box with a white spot.

9

2. If a box has a white spot on it, then you cannot stack it on a box with a red spot.

6 **Formal/Informal Language** Sitha uses formal language when she responds to Mr. Smith's question. How could she reply informally?

289

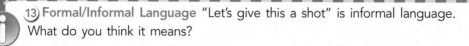

13 **Formal/Informal Language** "Let's give this a shot" is informal language. What do you think it means?

290

 20 **Expressions** "To think outside of the box" means "to think creatively or differently from most people."

Opening a
School Store

At a recent meeting, the parents' group at Mills Elementary School decided to open a school store. Their goal is to raise funds for extra activities and equipment the school cannot afford. Some parents have already formed a planning committee to discuss ideas.

Plan for a School Store

1. Find a good, central location.
2. Choose what **products** to sell.
3. Buy items from reliable suppliers.
4. Decide on prices of what we will sell.
5. Set up the space.
6. Determine store hours.
7. Train volunteer workers (including students).
8. Set up a page on the school's website.
9. Open for business.

Items to Sell

Supplies:

Notebooks	Rulers
Folders	Pens
Paper	Pencils
Glue	Colored Pencils
Tape	Markers
Scissors	

Apparel:

T-shirts
Baseball caps (for adults & youths)
Jackets
Backpacks

Report

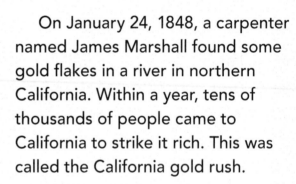

Gold Rush!

by Amanda Bleecker

On January 24, 1848, a carpenter named James Marshall found some gold flakes in a river in northern California. Within a year, tens of thousands of people came to California to strike it rich. This was called the California gold rush.

In 1848, California was not yet a state. It was a territory. Most of the population was Native American. By 1850, more than 300,000 gold seekers rushed to California from the rest of the United States and other countries. These people spoke many languages and had different religions and customs. More than 25,000 miners came from China!

In 1850, California became the 31st state of the United States.

Most of the miners who came to California had left their hometowns in a hurry. Many came with just the clothes on their backs. They needed food, housing, and other **supplies**. Very few women came to California. Some worked in restaurants and hotels.

The California gold rush reached its peak by 1852. After that, miners kept arriving, even though gold was difficult to find. Changes in mining technology made big **profits** for the mining companies. But these changes destroyed the landscape and drove many miners away.

By the end of the decade, the state's population had grown to 380,000.

Skagway, Alaska:

by Nick Skouras

In 1897, people in the United States heard great news. There was gold in the Pacific Northwest. When the *Portland* docked in Seattle, Washington, carrying a ton of gold, the rush was on. Soon thousands of people from all over the world headed for the little town of Skagway, Alaska. There, folks from all walks of life would begin their 600-mile trek to the goldfields of Canada's Klondike region. The people who made this trek were called "stampeders." The difficult journey stretched across the mountainous White Pass Trail to Bennett Lake. Stampeders then traveled by boat down the Yukon River to Dawson City. This makeshift town was built next to the

◀ gold rush miner

Gateway to Gold

goldfields. Were shiny gold nuggets lying around everywhere, just waiting to be found? That was the hope.

But gold seekers were not the only ones who flocked to Skagway. Some people came to provide goods and services to the miners. After all, they needed gear, food, and other supplies.

One person who decided early on not to **earn** money as a gold seeker was Harriet Pullen. She was determined to succeed in her own way. She needed to support her four children still back home in Washington.

Harriet's first employer was Captain William Moore, the founder of Skagway. He **hired** Mrs. Pullen as a cook for his pier-building crew. But in her spare time, Harriet collected empty tin cans and beat them into pie tins. It didn't take long before she was making extra money baking and selling homemade apple pies.

▼ Miners crossed the mountains behind the town of Skagway to find gold.

HEART OF THE KLONDIKE

As stampeders came and went, Harriet observed that most gold seekers were unprepared for the mountain journey. She also heard about overloaded pack animals dying along the steep trail. She learned that many trekkers spent months going back and forth, back and forth, carrying only a small load at one time. No wonder so many stampeders became sick due to lack of food and proper clothing.

Mrs. Pullen saw that money could be made moving gear and supplies over the White Pass Trail. She already owned seven strong workhorses back on her farm in Washington, so she brought them to Skagway. After obtaining some sturdy wagons, she set up her own freight hauling **business**. The company made up to $25 per day. That was a lot of money in those days. She transported freight for thousands of prospectors.

Prove It

What details show that Harriet Pullen was a good businesswoman?

By 1899, the need for freight haulers had lessened. After all, only a few stampeders ever found the riches they sought. Most of the 100,000 gold seekers who passed through Skagway came back empty-handed.

But Harriet Pullen was not one to sit idly by. Ever the **entrepreneur**, she bought Captain Moore's home and turned it into a hotel. And what a lovely inn it was. Pullen House Hotel became famous for its soft beds, fine china and silver, and even bathtubs. **Customers** flocked there. "Ma" Pullen, as she was called, became a big success. In fact, long after the Klondike gold rush was over, Harriet continued to welcome tourists and share tales of her amazing life.

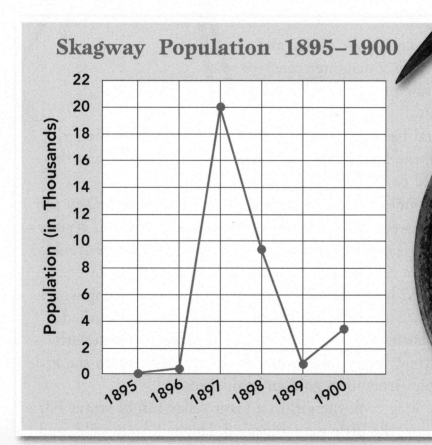

Skagway Population 1895–1900

Population (in Thousands)

1895 1896 1897 1898 1899 1900

▲ In 1896, very few people lived in Skagway, Alaska. After gold was discovered, thousands more people moved there.

Rumpelstiltskin: A Spin on the Usual Story

by Mia Lewis

One day a poor miller met the king. "My daughter can spin straw into gold!" the miller boasted.

"Send her to my palace," the king said. When the girl arrived, the king led her to a room full of straw. "Spin this into gold or die," he said, and left.

Of course, she could not spin straw into gold. When she began to weep, a little man appeared. "Why are you crying?" he asked. The girl explained. The little man said he would help if she could make him laugh. So she told her favorite jokes. And laugh he did. Then he sat at the spinning wheel and turned all the straw to gold. After that, he vanished.

At dawn, the king took the girl to a bigger room with more straw. "Spin gold or die," he demanded. Again the little man spun straw into gold and vanished.

The king took the girl to a giant cellar full of straw. For a third time, the little man appeared, laughed, spun gold, and then disappeared.

The greedy king was now in love…with his new gold. He wanted more. So he proposed marriage to the girl.

"Can I think about it?" she asked. The angry king locked her in the cellar. She began to cry, and once more the little man appeared. He helped her come up with a plan.

When the king returned, the little man greeted him. "Rumpelstiltskin is my name," he began, "and I spun the straw into gold, but—" The angry king lunged at him, but Rumpelstiltskin disappeared.

The miller's daughter came out from her hiding place. She explained everything. "But don't worry," she added. "Rumpel and I are going into business together. We're a great team, you know: he spins gold after he laughs. And only I can make him laugh."

The king knew that the **taxes** alone from such a business would keep him in gold. So, in the end, Rumpel-Miller, Inc., was born. And they earned happily ever after.

How I Saved Closets and Made Money

by Ellen Appelbaum

One day last month, I started dreaming about the new bike I wanted. I checked my **savings** and knew that I didn't have enough to pay for it. Then I read an article about kids who turned useful ideas into successful businesses.

"Can I earn the money I need?" I wondered.

Then Mom told me to clean my closet. At first I didn't want to, but then the chore gave me a great idea. Now I knew what business to start—a closet-cleaning business!

My parents thought it was a good idea, too, so we put our heads together and came up with a plan.

"You could **advertise**," said Mom. "You could make flyers to tell people about your business. Your brother Luis could help."

I knew I'd have to pay Luis, and that meant it would take longer to earn the money for my bike.

"How about it, bro?" I asked him, smiling hopefully. "For every dollar I make, I'll pay you forty cents. You could make a lot of money!"

"I won't clean, but I'll lift heavy stuff," he said.

Zoom In

What gave the narrator the idea to start his own closet-cleaning business? How do you know?

Next, I created a batch of flyers and then delivered them to our neighbors. Before long, customers started to call! Mom **loaned** us her cleaning supplies. I promised to repay her from my profits.

The following day we headed to our first job, at Mrs. Sanchez's house. She showed us the closet. It was really messy, and there were papers everywhere. Then the closet started ringing! I rapidly dug through the papers. Mrs. Sanchez grinned when I found the phone. Later she happily handed us the money we had agreed on.

$70.00 total
-$28.00 Luis
$42.00
-$5.00 expenses
$37.00 profit

The Chans' house was next. As we worked, Mr. Chan came in and stopped us. He is a sculptor. He turns unusual objects into art. Mr. Chan pulled old gym shoes from our bag. "This is useful stuff!" he said.

We earned more money that day, which added to our total. We were on a roll.

After cleaning five more closets that week, I added up my **income**. I repaid Mom $5 for supplies and paid Luis. I ended up with a $37 profit. I was able to save all of that money from the work I did, but it still wasn't enough. I needed enough for the cost of the bike plus the tax!

The next week I got four more customers. They had all seen my flyers. My advertising really paid off.

In all, I cleaned nine closets in six days. I knew that I had another profitable week. But it was time to do more paperwork. I might just have enough for the bike. Doing *this* kind of math was enjoyable!

| Week | Income | Expenses | | Profit |
		Paid to Luis	Cleaning Supplies	
1				
2				

After paying my **expenses**, I finally had enough money to buy the bicycle I wanted. I felt like a real success! I didn't want to carry all that cash to Bicycle Town, so we decided that Dad would use his credit card to pay for the bike, and I would pay Dad.

We all went to the store together to get the bike. The store was close enough to our house that I could ride my bike home.

"Mom, Dad, look!" I called as I passed them on my bike.

"There goes our entrepreneur!" my mom said proudly.

Prove It

What steps did the narrator have to take in order to buy his bike? Where did you find your answers?

Two for Tees

by Susan M. Meredith

Cast of Characters

IZZY **SARA,** Izzy's mom

SCENE 1

Setting: Saturday afternoon at 1:30 P.M. IZZY is helping her mother at home in the workroom where SARA operates her custom T-shirt business.

SARA: (*at the computer*) Izzy, could you pull out two white T-shirts from the closet?

IZZY: Sure, Mom. Do you want me to lay them flat on the table?

SARA: That would be great. I'm just finishing up the designs.

IZZY: (*looking over at the monitor*) Those colors look great together.

SARA: Thanks. Do you think the lettering stands out enough?

IZZY: Definitely.

SARA: Good. How is your design coming along?

IZZY: Well, I *thought* I was done. But Marta just texted me to say she wanted dark blue T-shirts instead of white.

SARA: Welcome to my world, Izzy. Customers ask for changes all the time.

IZZY: But Marta still wants her tees ready by Monday!

SARA: Don't worry. A box of dark shirts arrived last week.

IZZY: That's a relief.

SARA: But we'll need to pick up another package of transfer paper.

IZZY: I thought we had enough.

SARA: For light colors, not for darks.

IZZY: Yikes! Can we drive over to the arts and crafts store soon?

SARA: Not until we finish this current project and drop it off at the post office. I promised delivery by Tuesday.

IZZY: Well, I'll help in any way I can.

SARA: Okay, junior partner, you know the routine.

IZZY: *(taking out a sheet of transfer paper from its package)* I'll put this into the printer.

SARA: Great. I'll just flip the image and it will be ready to print.

(They both watch as the design prints out.)

SARA: Looks good. While I trim the transfer, why don't you get out the iron?

IZZY: Will do. I turn it on high, right?

SARA: Uh-huh. Then comes the tricky part.

IZZY: I know—HPT. Heat. Pressure. Time.

SARA: Yep. Use enough of each and everything turns out great. Let's do it!

Prove It

In what ways are Scene 1 and Scene 2 different? Tell how you know.

SCENE 2

Setting: Saturday afternoon at 4:00 P.M.; IZZY and SARA are just coming out of the arts and crafts store with their package of transfer paper.

SARA: Mission accomplished, Izzy!

IZZY: It was sure faster than I expected.

SARA: Same here. I've never seen such a short line at the post office.

IZZY: Look! The Snack Room doesn't have a big crowd in it, either.

SARA: Why don't we celebrate our hard work with something good to eat?

IZZY: Great idea.

The End

Minding My Own Business

as told by Kiran Shah to Lois Markam

Do you think owning a business would be fun? I think it's fun, but it's also hard work. I opened a vegetarian Indian restaurant. Now people who don't eat meat have a nice restaurant to go to. I serve traditional foods from my home country. Everything in my restaurant is freshly made. Nothing comes from a package.

When I first came to the United States, I worked as an engineer. However, I wanted my own business. "I'll open a restaurant," I thought. After all, I enjoy cooking. I learned to cook by watching my mother.

Starting a business costs money. You have to take **risks**, too. I had to rent a building, buy equipment, decorate, and buy food and supplies. For years before I opened my restaurant, I had saved money. I used those savings to begin my business. My family was able to loan me some money, too.

I also needed to get a business permit. To do that, I had to learn all the laws about restaurants. The state gives a useful class for people opening restaurants. I learned about such things as defrosting food safely and keeping my equipment clean.

THE COMMONWEALTH OF MASSACHUSETTS

FEE
$20.00

City of *Lowell*
Board of Health of

PERMIT TO OPERATE A FOOD ESTABLISHMENT

February 5, 2002

In accordance with Regulations promulgated under authority of Chapter 94, Section 305A and Chapter 111, Section 5 of the General Laws a Permit is hereby granted to:

Whose place of business is ..... *Omkar*
Type of business and any restrictions ..... *1717 Middlesex Street*
To operate a food establishment in ..... *Lowell, MA 01851*
(City of Town)

Permit Expires *December 31, 2002*

FORM 730 A.M. SULKIN COMPANY

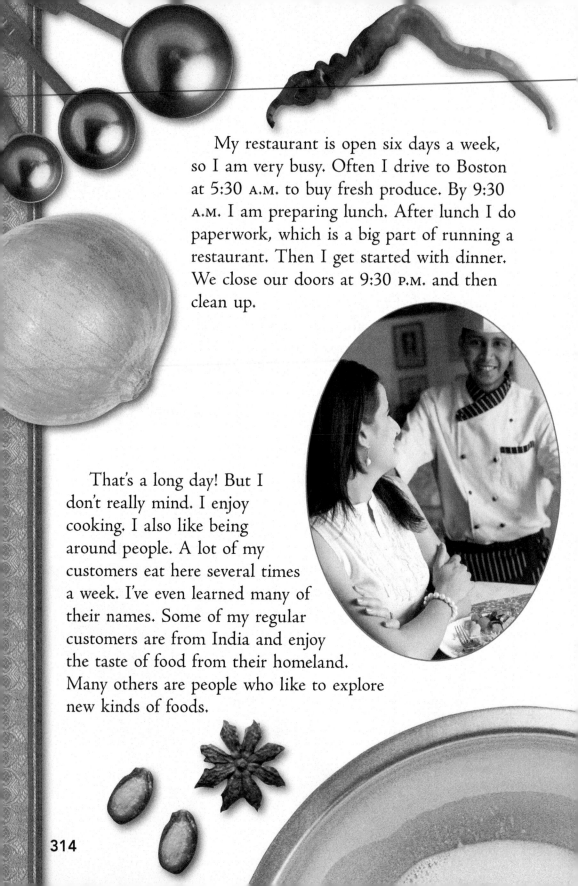

My restaurant is open six days a week, so I am very busy. Often I drive to Boston at 5:30 A.M. to buy fresh produce. By 9:30 A.M. I am preparing lunch. After lunch I do paperwork, which is a big part of running a restaurant. Then I get started with dinner. We close our doors at 9:30 P.M. and then clean up.

That's a long day! But I don't really mind. I enjoy cooking. I also like being around people. A lot of my customers eat here several times a week. I've even learned many of their names. Some of my regular customers are from India and enjoy the taste of food from their homeland. Many others are people who like to explore new kinds of foods.

Kiran Shah's Work Day

59% Cooking

7% cleanup

11% paperwork

23% shopping

Kiran spends most of his day cooking.

Right now, I have just one **employee** in my restaurant. But my family helps out, too. I work about 16 hours each day. Laws limit how much an employee can work, but an employer's hours are limitless!

I know that if my restaurant becomes more successful, I'll be able to hire more employees. Then I'll be able to work fewer hours each day.

I will probably never be rich, but I enjoy my work. That's worth a lot!

Prove It

From the pie chart, what things do you understand about owning a restaurant?

Starting a Food Business

by Frank Helfer

People like to eat. They like trying different foods, too. No wonder there are so many cooks, bakers, and snack-makers around. But starting a food business is not easy.

The first task is asking yourself some hard questions: What kind of food should I offer? How will my business be special? Who are my target customers? Where shall I locate? How many employees should I hire? How much will it cost to run my business? What taxes will I need to pay?

The answers to these questions must go into a business plan. This plan tells others that you are serious about your ideas. It lets investors know that lending you money will not be a big risk.

In a food business, you must follow many laws. They exist to ensure the safety and health of your customers and your workers.

Different kinds of food businesses have their own challenges. A small take-out shop often sells just a few kinds of items. So expenses will be lower than those of a big restaurant. Still, the food must be high quality. Otherwise customers will not return.

A mobile food truck has different challenges. The cost to set up the truck itself will be high at first. There should be room to store, cook, and serve your food. The menu must be unique enough to bring in customers. Another challenge is finding a place to park where lots of people pass by every day.

A home-based food business has its own needs. Let's say you are a cookie or snack maker. Your product must be better than the competition in some way. Also, you need to find creative ways to sell your goodies. Fortunately, your expenses will usually be low. You may not even need employees.

Prove It

What are some details that show how someone should start planning a food business?

Learn the Words

You're smart to keep your **savings** in the bank.

I'm a new **employee**. I want to save a part of my **income** each month.

employee
supplies
savings
loan
income
product
tax
expenses

- Read the words on the list.
- Read the dialogue.
- Find the words.

1. You Are the Reporter
Listening and Speaking

You are reporting on the opening of a new bank in your community. Prepare your news story. Tell how the bank can help local business people. Use at least one vocabulary word in your report. Read it to the class.

2. Write an Ad
Writing

Pretend that you have started a business. What is it? Write an ad for your business. Show it to a partner. See if anything can be made better in the ad.

3. Give a Speech
Listening and Speaking

Is there a store you would like to have in your community? Give a speech. Tell why this store would be important to your neighborhood. Give your opinions.

4. Take a Survey
Graphic Organizer

Ask 5 classmates which of the items below they would want to save up for. Tally their choices. Share your findings with your partner.

What Would You Save For?	
Music Player	
Bike	
Skates	
Computer Game	

Give It a Try

by Samantha Ruiz

Entrepreneurs can be found everywhere. Many of them are younger than 18—much younger. But age means little for those with big dreams. Some kid go-getters have a love of music or food or animals. Others carry on family traditions. Whatever their passion, these kids go for it.

Here are the stories of two entrepreneurs. They both have made a profit doing what they love.

Joe started a business called Pet Pals. He feeds pets and walks dogs. He got the idea when his neighbor went away. Joe took care of her hamster for a week. Now he gets paid for work that he loves. He created a website to advertise his business.

Maya makes memories. How does she do it? She makes scrapbooks for other people. Her work takes time, but her final product is beautiful. Each scrapbook is unique. Each one tells a story.

Maya charges by the page. She puts a sticker with her name on the back of the book. This is a good way to advertise. It brings more customers, and that means more income!

Maya is thinking of branching out into video scrapbooks. She's learning about computers and video cameras from her aunt. Pretty soon, Maya will be a multimedia entrepreneur.

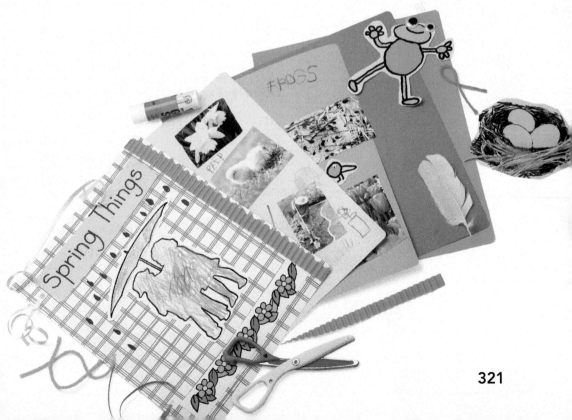

Pilar's Pet Hotel

Are you worried about caring for your pet while you are away from home? We can help!

We care for:

★ dogs

★ cats

★ small reptiles and mammals

★ birds

LOW RATES!

Insured Member of the National Pet Hotel Association

Member of the National Association of Professional Pet Sitters

Your pet will receive:
loving care, healthy food, daily exercise, a roomy cage, professional grooming

"I take my own pets to Pilar's Pet Hotel. I highly recommend it!"
—Dr. James Allen, veterinarian

Call today: 555-7799
or e-mail us at: pilarspethotel.nar

Retell "How I Saved Closets and Made Money"

> ℹ️ When you retell a story, you tell only the most important events. You can tell what the story's main problem is, and how the characters solve the problem. Words such as *problem*, *question*, and *puzzle* can tell about a problem. Words such as *then*, *so that*, and *solve* can tell about a solution.

"How I Saved Closets and Made Money" is realistic fiction. The main character has a problem, which he solves. Review the story on pages 302–307. Look at the pictures on page 325.

◼ Problem: What is the main character's problem?

◼ Events: How did the main character work on the problem? What did he do?

◼ Solution: How did things turn out for the boy?

Use the pictures on page 325 to retell the story to your partner. As you retell each part, point to the correct picture. Use complete sentences.

Words you might use in your retelling:		
business	profit	advertise
customer	earn	supplies

problem

$85.00

events

solution

325

Dig Deeper

Look Back

Work with a partner. Look at selections that tell about people running a business. Look at both informational articles and fiction. Find evidence that supports each statement below. List one piece of evidence for each statement. Each partner should write the answers on a sheet of paper.

1. A good business sells something that customers need.

2. A good business starts with a plan.

3. The owner of a business must usually work hard.

4. The owner must use some money to pay expenses.

Talk About It

The sneakers are blue.

The sneakers are blue and white.

The sneakers are blue and white with green laces.

The sneakers are blue and white with green laces and are comfortable.

Now it's your turn. With your classmates, tell about something else to wear. Add more and more details.

Conversation

 When people negotiate, they try to solve a problem. They listen to each other. They learn what each person wants. They try to agree in a way that helps both people.

Talk to a partner. One of you will be person A. The other will be person B.

Person A	Person B

Person A

Suggest how you and your partner can share one computer.

Person B

Disagree. Suggest another way to share it.

Reply. Explain why your solution is better.

Reply. Tell why your solution is better.

Agree.

Tell what you have both agreed to do.

Inside Our Bodies

The **BIG** Question

How do our bodies work?

☐ Which parts of our bodies help us breathe, eat, sleep, and think?

☐ Which muscle in our bodies works even when we are fast asleep?

☐ How can we keep our bodies strong and healthy?

What do different parts of our bodies do?

1. **What are some parts of your body?**

   In my body, I have…

   ☐ a heart.

   ☐ lungs.

   ☐ bones.

   ☐ a brain.

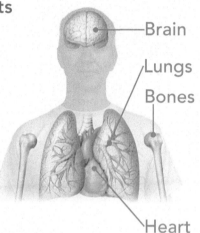

Brain

Lungs

Bones

Heart

2. **Why is it important to eat the right foods?**

   Eating well will…

   ☐ keep your muscles strong.

   ☐ keep your heart healthy.

   ☐ give you energy.

   ☐ fight off sickness.

3. **What does your heart do?**

My heart…

☐ beats.

☐ pumps blood.

☐ works day and night.

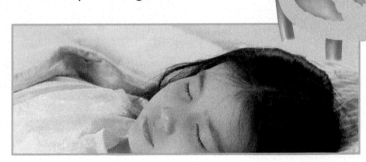

4. **What parts of your body give you strength?**

I am strong because of my…

☐ heart.

☐ muscles.

☐ bones.

☐ lungs.

Say **more!**

Theme Vocabulary

cell

tissue

organ

function

nervous system

control

brain

spinal cord

> ℹ The easiest way to remember the meaning of a new word is to use the word. As you discuss the human body, use these vocabulary words. Use them when you read and write about the body, too.
>
> **Read** the word.
> **Look** at the picture.
> **Listen** to your teacher.

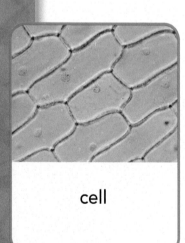

cell

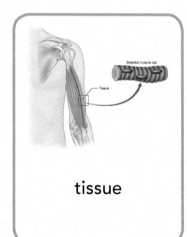

tissue

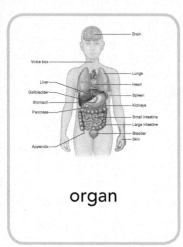

organ

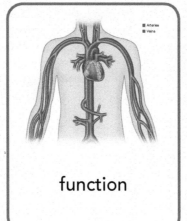

function

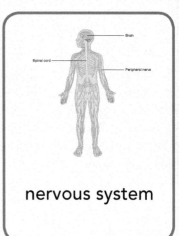

nervous system

control

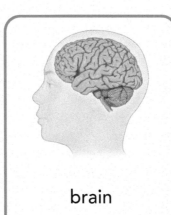

brain

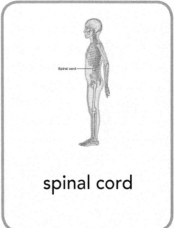

spinal cord

Which Picture?

Look at the vocabulary cards. Choose one picture. Don't tell anyone what it is! Describe the picture. See if your partner can guess which picture you chose.

4 **Formal/Informal Language** "Chill out" is an informal way to say "don't worry" or "relax." "I got this" is an informal way to say "I'm taking care of this."

17 **Formal/Informal Language** Calling someone a "wimp" is an insulting way of saying the person is weak and cowardly. Would you ever use this expression in a formal or polite conversation?

Let's Talk
About the Body!

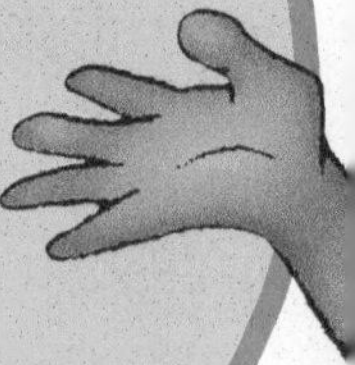

Everyone's body has the same important parts. However, people call these parts different things, depending on the language they speak.

When it comes to your body, good communication is very important. At the hospital or clinic, there might be a translator. The translator speaks two or more languages. He or she makes sure that the doctor and the patient understand one another. This can be very helpful, especially when you are not feeling well!

KEY

English
Spanish
Vietnamese
Cantonese

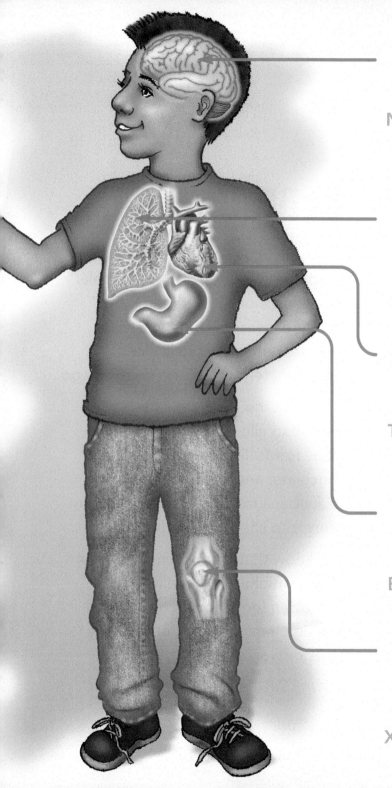

Brain
Cerebro
Não Bµ (now-bo)
Nou

Lungs
Pulmones
Ph±i (foe-ee)
Fai

Heart
Corazón
Trái tim (try tim)
Sam

Stomach
Estómago
Bao tØ (bow to)
Wai

Bones
Huesos
Xß_ng (sue-oong)
Gwat

Friendly Letter

July 20

Dear Adriana,

Thank you so much for inviting me to spend the summer in Guatemala! The photos of your grandparents' farm are awesome, and your grandparents look really nice. Unfortunately, there's no way I can go.

Here's the problem. I have really bad allergies. I am allergic to many foods (like milk, eggs, wheat, chocolate, and shellfish). Eating is tricky because some of the foods I'm allergic to show up in other foods.

I know that if I'm in an unfamiliar place, I might accidentally eat a forbidden food. I could have a bad reaction. I might break out in itchy hives or worse!

It's not such a big deal, though. My allergies haven't affected my attitude. I just know I won't be able to do some things I want to do, like travel.

Do you think you could explain all this to your grandparents? Tell them I wish I could visit them. I appreciate being invited!

Lots of love from your friend,

Sari

The Body's Organs

Different parts of our bodies help us breathe, think, sleep, eat, and stay healthy. Some of these parts are **organs** that work together in body systems. Each organ has a different **function**. The body systems work together so that we can be healthy, happy, and amazing.

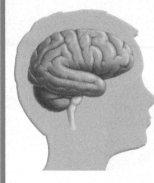

brain

The brain is part of the **nervous system**. It has over 100 billion nerve **cells**. The squishy gray brain **tissue** doesn't look like much, but it is the boss of you. The brain **controls** your movement, your breathing, and your thinking. Even your feelings and memories come from the brain. Exercise can help your brain stay sharp.

heart

The heart pushes blood through the body. It is part of the **circulatory system**. This important organ is a strong **muscle** that works all day and all night. A person's heart beats about 100,000 times a day, and 35 million times a year. Exercise helps keep your heart healthy.

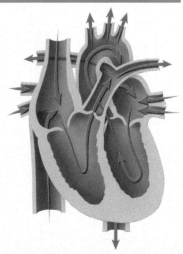

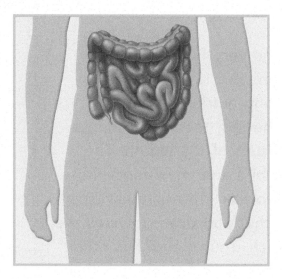

intestines

The intestines are part of the **digestive system**. When you eat food, the chewed up mixture goes down into your stomach. The stomach breaks down the food into a slushy mixture. The slushy mixture then passes through to the intestines. The intestines absorb all the good parts, or the nutrients, that we need from what we have eaten. The rest is passed on as waste. An adult's intestines are about 22 feet long.

lungs

Lungs are part of the **respiratory system**. The lungs take in oxygen from the air. They filter out carbon dioxide. Oxygen from the lungs goes to the rest of the body. When you breathe in, your lungs get bigger, like a balloon filling up with air. When you breathe out, your lungs get smaller. Your lungs also give you the power to talk, sing, and shout! Exercise helps to make your lungs stronger.

mouth

The mouth is the very first part of the digestive system. This is where the process of getting nutrients from food begins. The lips, teeth, and tongue are all part of the mouth. The teeth bite and chew food into small pieces. The tongue helps push the food down towards the stomach. Your mouth has other functions as well. Lips, teeth, and tongue are all important for speaking. You use your lips to smile, too.

nose

The nose is part of the respiratory system. When you breathe in through your nose, the air goes down through your nostrils and fills your lungs. Along the way, the air is cleaned, warmed, and made less dry. Dust, pollen, and germs in the air stick to mucus inside your nose. That helps your lungs stay clean so they can work properly. The nose also helps us smell and taste. Smell is important. For example, smelling smoke can warn you of danger.

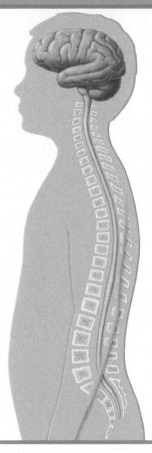

spinal cord

The **spinal cord** is part of the nervous system. It carries messages from the brain to the muscles. These messages control actions. The spinal cord starts at the base of the neck. It goes down the middle of the back. Nerves branch out from it towards all the parts of the body. The spinal cord is protected by the bones of the spine. The bones of the spine are shaped a bit like thick rings. Stacked together, the rings create a tunnel. The spinal cord runs up and down the inside of that tunnel.

stomach

The stomach is part of the digestive system. It stores and digests the food you have eaten. Digesting food means breaking it down. The stomach does that using gastric juices, and with strong muscles that squeeze and churn the food and the juices together. A person's stomach can hold up to four quarts of food.

Prove It

How would the organization of this article help you find information you are looking for?

MUSCLES DO THAT!

Muscles help you jog and jump.
Muscles cause your heart to pump.

Muscles help your arms to bend.
Oh, those muscles are your friends!

Muscles pull our arms out straight.
Hey, those muscles work just great!

Muscles help you wiggle toes,
Smile and laugh, and twitch your nose.

Muscles help you skip along,
Help you whistle, sing a song.

Muscles help you wink an eye,
And help your buddies wave good-bye!

by Binh Quang Nguyen

My Mouth

stays shut
       but
food just
finds
    a way

           my tongue says

we are
       full today
       but
           teeth just
              grin
       and
       say
              come in

i am always hungry

by Arnold Adoff

347

Your Busy Body

by Mario Jimenez

Do you know how your body works? To help understand how your body works, let's compare it to something that you know. You can think of the human body as a busy school.

At school, many things are happening at once. Teachers are teaching, and students are learning. A lot of things are going on, and people are moving around. Everyone must work together. It's the same with your body.

Compare your brain to your school's main office. The office is the control center of the school. Office workers guide the flow of information around the school. The principal guides the teachers and students.

Your brain controls your body just the same way. It sends messages to every part of your body. It also receives messages from different parts of the body. Your brain figures out what is going on. It tells the other parts of the body what to do every second of every day.

The brain has three main parts: the cerebrum, the cerebellum, and the brain stem.

Just as one student is leaving the office, another one is going in. They are all carrying important messages to and from the school's control center. The messages go to all parts of the school.

In your body, the nervous system carries messages. The messages travel from your brain to the parts of your body and back again.

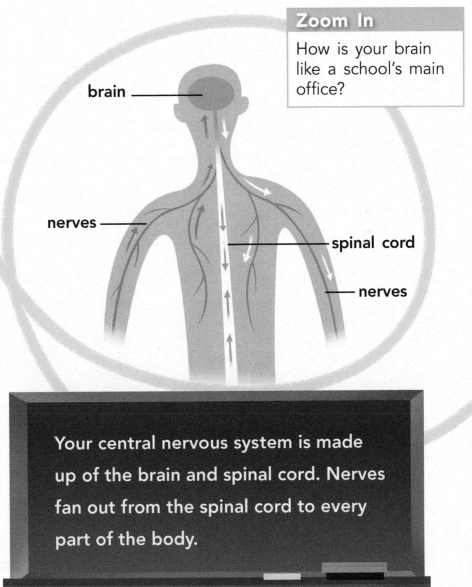

brain

nerves

spinal cord

nerves

Zoom In

How is your brain like a school's main office?

Your central nervous system is made up of the brain and spinal cord. Nerves fan out from the spinal cord to every part of the body.

Now let's look at the school building. Beneath the walls is a wooden or iron framework. This framework's base **supports** the walls and protects the pipes and wires.

Your **skeletal system** is a little bit like the base of the school. It supports your body and gives it shape. It also protects the organs inside your body.

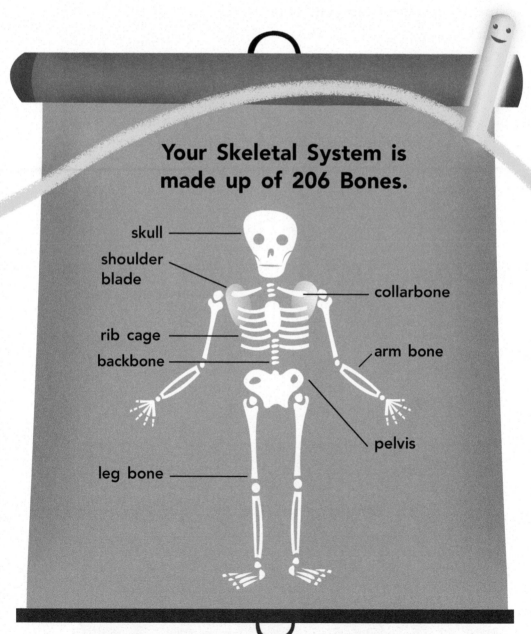

Your Skeletal System is made up of 206 Bones.

skull

shoulder blade

collarbone

rib cage

backbone

arm bone

pelvis

leg bone

Prove It

What does the author compare the human body to?

In a school, children go from one room to the next. They may go to the library or to the gym. Similarly, blood flows through your body. How does it get around? Your heart pumps it. It goes to each part of your body and back again.

As you can see, your body and your school are both very busy places. Speaking of school, I'd better get back to class!

heart

veins

artery

In your circulatory system, arteries carry blood and oxygen from your heart. Blood returns to your heart through **veins**.

353

TOP SEVEN THINGS YOUR BLOOD DOES FOR YOU!

by Diane Brye

1. It feeds you.

The food you eat wouldn't do you any good without your blood. Your teeth bite and chew your food. Your tongue helps you swallow it. Your stomach digests it. Your intestine absorbs the nutrients that your body needs. But it is the blood that takes those nutrients where they need to go. Blood travels through your arteries. It takes nutrients to each and every cell in your body. Without your blood, your cells would go hungry.

2. It takes out the trash.

Just as your body's cells always need fresh nutrients, they also need to get rid of their waste. That's another job for your blood. Blood cells traveling back from delivering food take away the cell's waste products. Blood that is carrying waste travels through your veins. The blood is then filtered to remove the waste.

3. It helps your cells breathe.

Cells throughout your body need oxygen. You breathe it in through your lungs. But how does oxygen get from the lungs to all your cells? The blood does this job. It carries oxygen through the circulatory system so that every cell can get what it needs. The blood also picks up waste gas in the form of carbon dioxide.

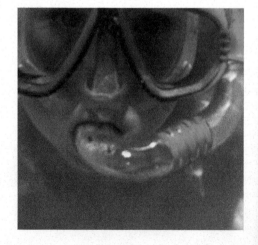

4. It clots.

When you have a cut or an injury, blood vessels are broken. The circulatory system starts to leak. Blood flows out. Your body needs a way to stop the bleeding fast! Special blood cells make the blood thicken and harden into a clot. This clot plugs the cut and stops the bleeding.

5. It fights invaders.

Sometimes your body is invaded by viruses or bacteria. (Another name for these is germs.) Any of these germs might make you sick. Your blood helps to fight off the invasion. White blood cells rush to the scene. Some "eat" the invaders. Others make proteins that attack the invaders.

6. It remembers.

Special proteins made by your white blood cells "remember" invading viruses or bacteria. The next time your body is attacked by the same invader, your white blood cells remember. This means they can respond more quickly. That's what happens when you get a shot. You are given a weak or inactive version of a disease germ. Your white blood cells make a "record" of the germ. Now you are ready to fight when the actual germ invades your body.

7. It sounds the alarm.

Life was dangerous for our ancestors way back when they lived by hunting and gathering. At any moment, they had to be ready to fight an enemy or run for their lives. Blood carries a substance that gives your body the strength to fight or run. It's called adrenaline. Today, adrenaline is more likely to make you feel a little nervous before you take a test or swing at a baseball.

Prove It

What are two details that show how blood helps every cell in your body?

357

Visiting Chef Jeff's Nose

by Joanne Wachter

Hi! We are Mr. and Mrs. Smell. I'm Spicy and this is Sweet. Here are our children, Tangy and Peppery. Pleased to meet you!

Our family loves to travel. We visit a lot of noses. We find that journeys inside noses are fun, exciting, and rewarding! Let me share some pictures of our latest trip. This time we went to see a pot of bubbly, hot chili.

Our trip started when famous Chef Jeff leaned over the pot of chili to take a whiff. As he sniffed in deeply, we were sucked into his nostrils. Soon we were zooming up into his nasal cavity. It was as warm and moist as a rain forest in there.

nostril

we are here
10:15:00

Our next stop was one of the special areas on the roof of the nasal cavity. These patches of skin tissue sense the specks of gas that make up smells. They can recognize many different smells.

The smell patches are not very big. They are about the size of a dime or a thumbnail, but they contain 10 million or more cells. These cells are what cause the brain to recognize smells. Your brain can recognize about 10,000 different odors. We just hoped that chili was one of the ones Chef Jeff would recognize and enjoy!

Zoom In

What happens first after Chef Jeff sniffs the chili?

cilia, mucus

we are here
10:15:02

Sticky stuff covers the smell patches and the whole inside of the nose. I've heard it is called mucus. It's easy to get caught in it! That's the point. You see, the mucus inside the nasal cavity traps anything other than air. It traps all the stuff that you don't want going down into your lungs. That could be dust, pollen, or bacteria.

We played in the sticky mucus for a while. Then we discovered something even more fun. They were little hairs called cilia. Oh, that tickles! Cilia stuck out of the mucus. They waved back and forth, helping us move along.

We couldn't stay long, though. We hurried to the olfactory bulbs. These bunches of nerves sent our messages to Chef Jeff's brain. Soon we heard him say, "Wow! This chili smells great!" Then he breathed out, and our journey was over. We were so happy that we had pleased him.

Our Smell family trips are quick. They last only a few seconds. It doesn't take us long to travel from the nose to the brain. We have lots of fun, especially when we get a compliment like the one from Chef Jeff!

olfactory bulbs send messages to brain

we are here
10:15:03

Prove It

What did Chef Jeff say when he smelled the chili? Where did you find your answer?

What Was That Again?

by Elisa Ann Suzuki

A baby crying, popcorn popping, a dog barking. Soft or loud, your ears let you hear the sounds around you. Inside your ear, there are several steps to turning sounds into signals that our brains can recognize.

It all starts with a sound. A girl near you claps her hands, for example. This creates sound waves that travel through the air. In less than a second, those sound waves hit your outer ear. The outer ear is on the outside of your head. Its main job is to collect sound waves. It funnels the sound waves into your ear canal. The ear canal makes the sounds louder.

Now the sounds are ready to move on to the middle ear. It's the middle ear's job to take the sound waves and turn them into vibrations. At the entrance of the middle ear is the eardrum. This thin piece of skin is stretched tight like a drum. Sound waves hitting the eardrum make it vibrate.

How We Hear Sounds

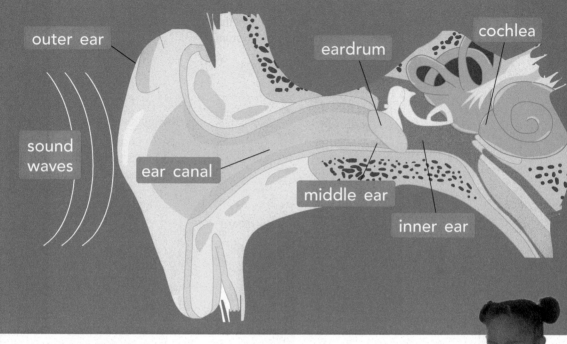

outer ear

cochlea

eardrum

sound waves

ear canal

middle ear

inner ear

Behind the eardrum are three tiny bones. The vibrating eardrum makes these bones move. Their movement carries the sound vibrations into the inner ear.

Inside the inner ear is a small curled tube that looks a bit like a snail shell. It is called the cochlea. The sound vibrations enter the cochlea. The cochlea is filled with liquid. The vibrations make the liquid inside the cochlea move. There are also little hairs on the walls of the cochlea. The vibrations make the hairs move as well.

Now it's time to send a message! A special nerve connects the cochlea to the brain. A message about the movement in the cochlea is sent to the brain as quickly as possible. The brain understands the message as sound. At last, you hear the girl clapping. Hooray! You can clap if you want to.

Learn the Words

X-RAY

This file is about my patient's **digestive system**.

I learned about the biggest **vein** in the **circulatory system**.

I know that, too. It's the vein that leads to the heart.

This is the X-ray of Mr. Lee's **lungs**. His **respiratory system** is just fine!

circulatory system
vein
respiratory system
lungs
skeletal system
support
muscle
digestive system

- Read the words on the list.
- Read the dialogue.
- Find the words.

1. You Are the Actor
Listening and Speaking

Work with a partner. Take turns reading the dialogue in the picture above. Use your best acting voice. Make the dialogue come alive. Ask your partner questions about any words you don't understand.

2. Dialogue
Listening and Speaking

Pretend you have hurt yourself. Take turns with your partner. Tell what is wrong. Explain what hurts.

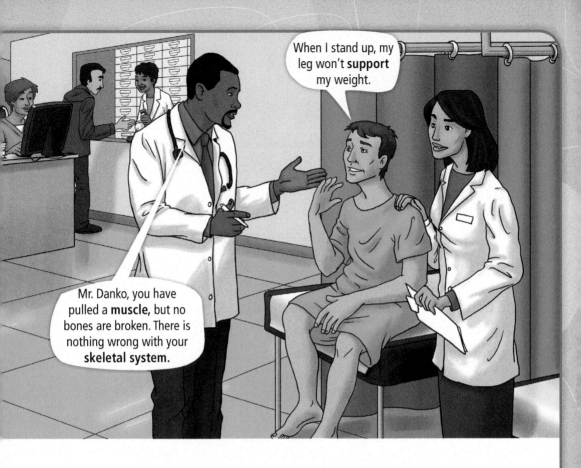

When I stand up, my leg won't **support** my weight.

Mr. Danko, you have pulled a **muscle,** but no bones are broken. There is nothing wrong with your **skeletal system.**

3. You Are the Writer
Writing

Pretend you are a doctor like the ones in the picture. Write an e-mail to a friend. Tell how you helped at least two people at the hospital today.

4. Make a Venn Diagram
Graphic Organizer

Work with a partner. Think of foods that each of you like. Fill in the Venn diagram. In the middle, put foods you both like.

Our Favorite Foods

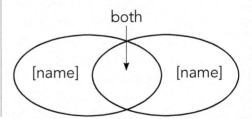

both

[name]   [name]

Measuring Your Heart Rate

by Lisa Shulman

Which muscle is always working? Your heart! It pumps blood whether you are swimming, sleeping, jumping, dancing, or reading this book. Your heart pumps blood to every part of your body. The blood brings your cells oxygen and nutrients. It also takes away waste. Sometimes your body needs more oxygen. Sometimes it needs less.

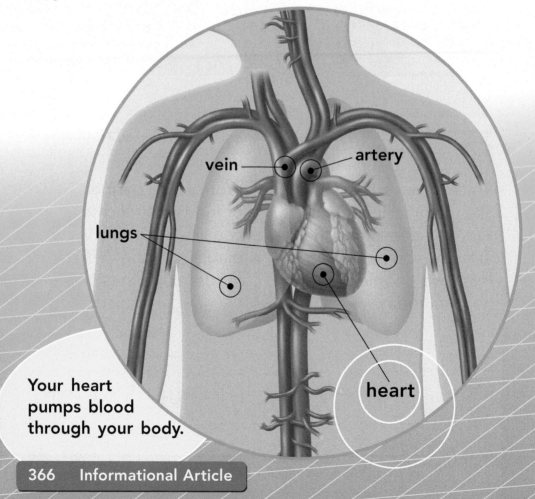

vein — artery

lungs

heart

Your heart pumps blood through your body.

Your heart pumps at different speeds at different times, according to what your body needs. It pumps faster and sends more blood to your muscles when they are busy. That's because when your muscles are active, they need more oxygen. Your heart pumps slower and sends less blood to your muscles when they are resting.

What Makes Your Heart Race?

Exercise makes your heart beat faster. But other things can as well.

+ If you are scared or excited, your body produces the hormone adrenaline. Adrenaline makes your heart beat faster.
+ If you are sick and have a fever, your heart beats faster. This is to bring more blood to your skin so it can cool down.
+ After a meal, your heart beats faster while you digest.
+ Some things that people eat or drink can make the heart beat faster, such as coffee or some medicines.

Measure Your Resting Heart Rate

1. Sit down for 7–10 minutes.
2. Put two fingers on your wrist.
3. Count the beats you feel in 10 seconds.
4. Multiply that number by 6.

Prove It

What is the first thing you need to do when you want to measure your active heart rate?

The Heart of an Athlete

Not everyone's heart beats at the same speed. During exercise, an athlete's heart beats more slowly than most. This is because an athlete's heart is very strong and fit! A stronger heart can pump more blood with each beat. That means it doesn't need to beat as many times to get the same amount of blood to the muscles.

If you are working out and getting in shape, over time, your active heart rate will go down. This is because your heart is getting stronger!

Measure Your Active Heart Rate

1. Exercise for 15 minutes. Then stop.
2. Put two fingers on your wrist.
3. Count the beats you feel for 10 seconds.
4. Multiply that number by 6.

Normal Resting Heart Rate

Age Group	Beats per Minute
babies	140
10-year-olds	70 to 120
children over 10 and adults	60 to 100

Heart-Smart Garden Soup

Looking for the best foods to keep your heart healthy and strong? Here's a short list of some of the best heart-healthy foods.

- black beans, kidney beans, lentils, or peas
- fruits and vegetables, such as apples, blueberries, carrots, spinach, broccoli, and tomatoes
- salmon, tuna, and sardines
- almonds, walnuts, pecans, or hazelnuts
- oatmeal, brown rice, tofu, and dark chocolate

This recipe for homemade soup uses heart-smart foods.

1 tablespoon vegetable oil

1 small yellow onion

1 clove of garlic

1 medium zucchini

1 small green pepper

1 can vegetable broth ($10\frac{1}{2}$ oz.)

$1\frac{1}{2}$ cups of water

1. Ask an adult to help you with the chopping and cooking.
2. Wash and chop all the vegetables.
3. Heat the oil in a large pot.
4. Cook the onion and the garlic in the oil until they are soft.
5. Add the vegetables, water, and broth.
6. Cook on medium heat for about 15 minutes.
7. Add salt and pepper to taste.

Retell "Your Busy Body"

> When you retell a selection, you give only the most important details and ideas. Sometimes you can compare and contrast to make the ideas easy to understand. Use words such as *just like*, *same as*, *however*, and *but* in your retelling.

"Your Busy Body" compares systems of the human body to what goes on in a school. Review the selection on pages 348–353. Look at the pictures on page 373.

■ First Row: What body system is described? How is it compared to a school?

■ Second Row: What system is described? How is it compared?

■ Third Row: What system is described? How is it compared?

Use the pictures on page 373 to retell the selection to your partner. As you retell each part, point to the correct pair of pictures. Use complete sentences.

Words you might use in your retelling:		
brain	spinal cord	skeletal system
function	vein	control

school

human body

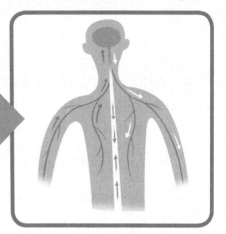

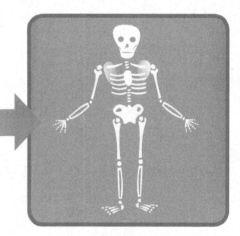

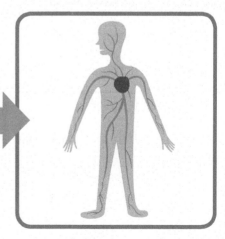

Dig Deeper

Look Back

Work with a partner. Look though the unit for information about the heart. Use that infomation to find the answers to these questions.

1. Why does your heart rate change?

2. What body system is your heart a part of?

3. How can you measure your heart rate?

4. What does your heart do to your blood?

Each partner should write the answers on a sheet of paper. Also write the page where you found your evidence.

Talk About It

Choose an object such as an orange.

What does it look like?

What does it smell like?

How does it feel?

How does it taste?

Come up with as many words as you can to describe the orange.

Conversation

 Sometimes a friend asks you how to do something. Then you need to give clear instructions. Always give each step in order. Use words like *first, second, next,* and *finally.*

Talk to a partner. One of you will be person A. The other will be person B.

Person A

Tell the first step of how to do something.

Tell the next step.

Give the correct third step if your partner was wrong.

Person B

Ask what you need to do next.

Guess the third step. Tell your partner.

Thank your partner.

GLOSSARY

ancestor

A

ad·ap·ta·tion (ăd′ăp-tā′shən) *n.* the change made to fit a different place or different conditions

ad·ver·tise (ăd′vər-tīz′) *v.* to tell people about a product or service that they can buy

ag·ri·cul·ture (ăg′rĭ-kŭl′chər) *n.* the science of growing crops and raising animals for food

al·ter (ôl′tər) *v.* to make something different

an·ces·tor (ăn′sĕs′tər) *n.* a person in your family or culture who lived a long time ago, before you were born

ar·rive (ə-rīv′) *intr.v.* to reach the place you wanted to go

B

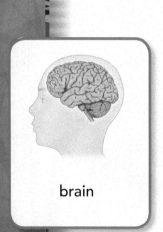

brain

bone (bōn) *n.* the hard material under the skin of animals and humans that helps form their bodies

brain (brān) *n.* the organ that controls most of the things the body does

ă pat / ā pay / âr care / ä father / ĕ pet / ē bee / ĭ pit / ī pie / îr pier / ŏ pot / ō toe / ô paw /

break down (brāk) (doun) *v.* to break something into smaller pieces

bur·ied (bĕr′ēd) *tr.v.* hidden or covered up, usually underground

busi·ness (bĭz′nĭs) *n.* a person or group of people who makes things and sells them for money, or who is paid to do things for others

business

C

cam·ou·flage (kăm′ə-fläzh′) *n.* the way an animal's color or shape helps it look like its surroundings

can·o·py (kăn′ə-pē) *n.* the layer of a rain forest where the leaves and branches of trees grow close together and block out the sunlight

can·yon (kăn′yən) *n.* a large valley surrounded by steep walls of rock

canyon

cap·i·tal (kăp′ĭ-tl) *n.* a city where a country's main government is located

cave (kāv) *n.* a large hole underground or in the side of a hill or mountain

cell (sĕl) *n.* the smallest living part that makes up living things

oi noise / o͝o took / o͞o boot / ou out / ŭ cut / ûr firm / hw which / th thin / *th* this / zh vision / ə about, item, edible, gallop, circus

cir·cu·la·to·ry sys·tem (sûr′kyə-lə-tôr′ē) (sĭs′təm) *n.* all the tissues and organs that move blood around the body

clas·si·fy (klăs′ə-fī′) *tr.v.* to sort into groups of things that are alike

cliff (klĭf) *n.* a high, steep area of rock, often at the edge of a sea or ocean

coast (kōst) *n.* the land that is next to the sea or ocean

compare

com·pare (kəm-pâr′) *v.* to look at how things are alike and how they are different

con·flict (kŏn′flĭkt′) *n.* a fight or disagreement between two people or groups

con·quer (kŏng′kər) *v.* to take control, sometimes by fighting

con·quis·ta·dor (kŏng-kē′stə-dôr′) *n.* a Spanish explorer

culture

con·trol (kən-trōl′) *v.* to be in charge of, or to have power over, something

cul·ture (kŭl′chər) *n.* the ideas, beliefs, and way of life of a group of people

ă pat / ā pay / âr care / ä father / ĕ pet / ē bee / ĭ pit / ī pie / îr pier / ŏ pot / ō toe / ô paw /

cus·tom (kŭs′təm) *n.* something that people have done in the same way for a long time

cus·tom·er (kŭs′tə-mər) *n.* a person who buys goods and services

D

dep·o·si·tion (dĕp′ə-zĭ′shən) *n.* a buildup of material that happens when water, wind, or ice drops rocks or soil in a new location

di·ges·tive sys·tem (dī-jĕs′tĭv) (sĭs′təm) *n.* the organs in the body that take in and break down food

dis·cov·er (dĭ-skŭv′ər) *v.* to find or learn something that was not known or seen before

dis·solve (dĭ-zŏlv′) *v.* to break down and become part of a liquid

di·ver·si·ty (dĭ-vûr′sĭ-tē) *n.* the many different kinds of things or people found in the world

E

earn (ûrn) *v.* to make money for doing work or providing a service

e·co·sys·tem (ē′kō-sĭs′təm) *n.* the plants, the animals, and the place where they live, and how they depend on one another

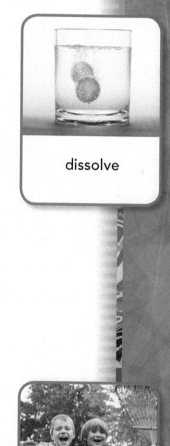

dissolve

earn

oi noise / ŏŏ took / ōō boot / ou out / ŭ cut / ûr firm / hw which / th thin / *th* this / zh vision / ə about, item, edible, gallop, circus

ed·u·ca·tion (ĕj′ə-kā′shən) *n.* the teaching and learning that goes on in schools

ef·fect (ĭ-fĕkt′) *n.* a change that is caused by something

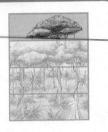

emergent layer

e·mer·gent lay·er (ĭ-mûr′jənt) (lā′ər) *n.* the highest layer of a rain forest

em·pire (ĕm′pīr′) *n.* a large group of territories that is controlled by one ruler

em·ploy·ee (ĕm-ploi′ē) *n.* a person who works for a person or company

em·ploy·ment (ĕm-ploi′mənt) *n.* the job a person has

en·coun·ter (ĕn-koun′tər) *v.* to meet a person or thing without expecting to

en·tre·pre·neur (ŏn′trə-prə-nûr′) *n.* someone who owns his or her own business

e·ro·sion (ĭ-rō′zhən) *n.* what happens when water, wind, or ice moves rocks and soil away

exhibit

ex·hib·it (ĭg-zĭb′ĭt) *n.* an object or objects put in a public place for people to see

ex·pens·es (ĭk-spĕns′ĭz) *n.pl.* things that people spend money on in daily life

ă pat / ā pay / âr care / ä father / ĕ pet / ē bee /
ĭ pit / ī pie / îr pier / ŏ pot / ō toe / ô paw /

ex·plor·er (ĭk-splôr′ər) *n.* someone who travels to an unknown place

ex·tinct (ĭk-stĭngkt′) *adj.* no longer alive in the world

F

fea·ture (fē′chər) *n.* something important, interesting, or typical of a place

food chain (fo͞od) (chān) *n.* when each animal becomes food for the next animal

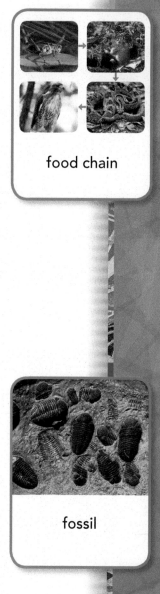

food chain

force (fôrs) *n.* something or someone that has a lot of power

for·est floor (fôr′ĭst) (flôr) *n.* the ground and any small plants that are close to the ground in a rain forest

fos·sil (fŏs′əl) *n.* what is left of a plant or animal after many years, when it has turned to rock

fossil

free·dom (frē′dəm) *n.* the right to say and do what you want

func·tion (fŭngk′shən) *n.* the job that something is supposed to do

oi **noise** / o͝o **took** / o͞o **boot** / ou **out** / ŭ **cut** / ûr **firm** / hw **which** /
th **thin** / *th* **this** / zh **vision** / ə **about, item, edible, gallop, circus**

G

ge·og·ra·phy (jē-ŏg′rə-fē) *n.* the study of Earth's surface and the countries of the world

ge·ol·o·gy (jē-ŏl′ə-jē) *n.* the study of Earth's rocks, soil, and landforms

gla·cier (glā′shər) *n.* a large piece of ice that moves slowly down a valley

glacier

H

har·vest (här′vĭst) *v.* to gather or pick a crop

hire (hīr) *v.* to pay someone to do work for you

home·land (hōm′lănd′) *n.* the country where a person was born

hu·mid (hyōō′mĭd) *adj.* damp, containing water or water vapor

I

i·den·ti·fy (ī-dĕn′tə-fī′) *v.* to say what something is

homeland

im·mi·grant (ĭm′ĭ-grənt) *n.* a person who leaves his or her country to go and live in a new country

in·come (ĭn′kŭm′) *n.* the money people earn for doing work or from owning a business

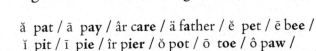
ă pat / ā pay / âr care / ä father / ĕ pet / ē bee /
ĭ pit / ī pie / îr pier / ŏ pot / ō toe / ô paw /

in·dus·try (ĭn′dəs-trē) *n.* the work of making things, especially in factories

in·tro·duce (ĭn′trə-dōōs′) *v.* to help someone learn about someone else, or something, for the first time

is·land (ī′lənd) *n.* a piece of land that is completely surrounded by water

island

L

la·bel (lā′bəl) *n.* a piece of paper that tells what something is

land·form (lănd′fôrm′) *n.* a natural feature on Earth's surface

land use (lănd) (yōōs) *n.* how most of the land in a place is used

lan·guage (lăng′gwĭj) *n.* the words that people use to speak to one another

lay·er (lā′ər) *n.* an amount of something that lies on top of something else or between other things

language

loan (lōn) *n.* to give someone something that will need to be given back or repaid later

lungs (lŭngz) *n.* organs in the body that are necessary to breathe

oi **n**oise / ŏŏ t**oo**k / ōō b**oo**t / ou **ou**t / ŭ c**u**t / ûr f**ir**m / hw **wh**ich / th **th**in / *th* **th**is / zh vi**s**ion / ə **a**bout, it**e**m, ed**i**ble, gall**o**p, circ**u**s

M

mus·cle (mŭs′əl) *n.* tissues in the body that help the body move and stretch

N

Native American

Na·tive A·mer·i·can (nā′tĭv) (ə-mĕr′ĭ-kən) *n.* one of a group of people who were the first to live in the Americas

nerv·ous sys·tem (nûr′vəs) (sĭs′təm) *n.* the brain, nerve cells, and nerve tissue working together to carry messages to and from the brain

O

op·por·tu·ni·ty (ŏp′ər-tōō′nĭ-tē) *n.* a chance to do something

or·gan (ôr′gən) *n.* a part of a living thing that performs a particular job

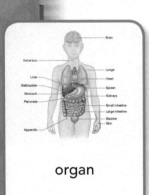

organ

P

pa·le·on·tol·o·gist (pā′lē-ŏn-tŏl′ə-jĭst) *n.* a person who studies fossils

plain (plān) *n.* a large area of flat land that has few trees

pred·a·tor (prĕd′ə-tər) *n.* an animal that lives by killing and eating other animals

ă pat / ā pay / âr care / ä father / ĕ pet / ē bee / ĭ pit / ī pie / îr pier / ŏ pot / ō toe / ô paw /

pre·his·tor·ic (prē′hĭs-tôr′ĭk) *adj.* the time in history before people started writing things down

pre·serve (prĭ-zûrv′) *v.* to keep something from being hurt or changed

prey (prā) *n.* an animal that is hunted as food by another animal

pro·cess (prŏ′sĕs′) *n.* a series of changes that happen naturally

pro·duce (prə-dōōs′) *v.* to make or create things, especially goods that will be sold

prod·uct (prŏd′əkt) *n.* something that is made or grown, and then sold

prof·it (prŏf′ĭt) *n.* the money that is left after a business buys its supplies and pays its bills

pro·tect (prə-tĕkt′) *v.* to keep something safe from harm

pro·vide (prə-vīd′) *v.* to give something that is needed or wanted

predator

protect

oi noise / ŏŏ took / ōō boot / ou out / ŭ cut / ûr firm / hw which / th thin / *th* this / zh vision / ə about, item, edible, gallop, circus

R

re·gion (rē′jən) *n.* one of the areas that a country is divided into

re·lat·ed (rĭ-lāt′ĭd) *v.tr.* when two people or animals are in the same family

re·li·gion (rĭ-lĭ′jən) *n.* a set of beliefs usually involving a belief in God or gods

religion

res·pi·ra·to·ry sys·tem (rĕs′pə-rə-tô′rē) (sĭs′təm) *n.* all the parts of the body that are used for breathing

risk (rĭsk) *n.* the possibility that something bad or dangerous may happen

ru·ins (rōō′ĭns) *n.pl.* the parts of a building or city that are left after it has been burned or knocked down

rul·er (rōōl′ər) *n.* a person who leads a country or group of people

ruins

S

sav·ings (sāv′ĭngs) *n.pl.* the money that people have earned but do not want to spend right away

seek (sēk) *v.* to search, or look, for something

ă pat / ā pay / âr care / ä father / ĕ pet / ē bee /
ĭ pit / ī pie / îr pier / ŏ pot / ō toe / ô paw /

set·tle (sĕt′l) *v.* to make a home in a new place

shore (shôr) *n.* the land at the edge of a sea, ocean, or lake

sight (sīt) *n.* an interesting place that people often visit

site (sīt) *n.* a place where something happened, or a place that is used for something

skel·e·tal sys·tem (skĕl′ĭ-tl) (sĭs′təm) *n.* all the bones that hold together the bodies of humans and many animals

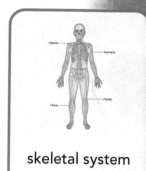

skeletal system

skel·e·ton (skĕl′ĭ-tn) *n.* all of the bones that fit together to support the body of a person or animal

skull (skŭl) *n.* the bone in the head of a person or animal that protects the brain

sol·dier (sōl′jər) *n.* someone who is in a country's army

soldier

spi·nal cord (spī′nəl) (kôrd) *n.* a thick string of nerve tissue down the back protected by bones of the spine

strug·gle (strŭg′əl) *v.* to try very hard to do something that is difficult

oi noise / ŏŏ took / ōō boot / ou out / ŭ cut / ûr firm / hw which / th thin / *th* this / zh vision / ə about, item, edible, gallop, circus

sup·plies (sə-plīs′) *n.* things that employees of a business need so they can do their jobs

sup·port (sə-pôrt′) *v.* to hold up or keep in place

support

T

tax (tăks) *n.* money that people pay to the government

ter·ri·to·ry (tĕr′ĭ-tôr′ē) *n.* a piece of land that belongs to a country or government

tis·sue (tĭsh′ōō) *n.* a group of cells that combine together

tour·ist (tŏŏr′ĭst) *n.* someone who travels and visits places

trade (trād) *n.* the act of giving another person something, and receiving something from the person in exchange

tra·di·tion (trə-dĭ′shən) *n.* something that people have done in the same way for a long time

treat·ment (trēt′mənt) *n.* how we act toward someone

trop·i·cal (trŏp′ĭ-kəl) *adj.* hot and wet, usually describing a place on Earth

trade

ă pat / ā pay / âr care / ä father / ĕ pet / ē bee /
ĭ pit / ī pie / îr pier / ŏ pot / ō toe / ô paw /

U

un·der·sto·ry (ŭn′dər-stôr′ē) *n.* a hot and wet layer in the rain forest, above the forest floor

V

val·ley (văl′ē) *n.* an area of low land between mountains

valley

vein (vān) *n.* a small tube in the body that carries blood to the heart

voy·age (voi′ĭj) *n.* a long journey by ship

W

weath·er·ing (wĕth′ər-ĭng) *v.tr.* what happens when wind, heat, water, or ice causes rocks or soil to break into smaller pieces

voyage

oi noise / ŏŏ took / ōō boot / ou out / ŭ cut / ûr firm / hw which / th thin / *th* this / zh vision / ə about, item, edible, gallop, circus

Acknowledgments

Text Acknowledgments: Excerpt from "The First Discovery" from *Journey to the Bottomless Pit: The Story of Stephen Bishop and Mammoth Cave* by Elizabeth Mitchell. Text copyright © 2004 by Betsy Mitchell. Reprinted by permission of Penguin Young Readers Group, a division of Penguin Group (USA) Inc.

Excerpt from "Grace Blasts Off" from *Starring Grace* by Mary Hoffman. Text copyright © 2000 by Mary Hoffman. Reprinted by permission of Puffin Books, a division of Penguin Group (USA) Inc.

"My Mouth" from *Eats* by Arnold Adoff. Text copyright © 1979 by Arnold Adoff. Reprinted by permission of Arnold Adoff.

"Snow," "Lessons," and an excerpt from "Father" from *Home of the Brave* by Katherine Applegate. Text copyright © 2007 by Katherine Applegate. Reprinted by permission of Feiwel and Friends, a division of Macmillan Children's Publishing Group.

Illustration Credits: Joseph Fiedler; Laurie Keller; Tom Newsom; Lizzy Rockwell; Alexandria Steel-Morgan; Karen Blessen; Richard Downs; Franklin Hammond; David McCall Johnston; Tony Klassen; Jason O'Malley; Kevin Rechin; Sachiko Yoshikawa; Bill Cigliano; Brian Fujimori; Todd Leonardo; Laura Ovresat; Tristan Elwell; Laura Ovresat; Tana Powell; John Sandford; Chris Lensch; Mike Reagan; Patrice Rossi-Calkin; Francesco Santalucia; Stacey Schuett; Suling Wang; Linda Holt-Ayriss; Josée Massé; Jason O'Malley; Michael Wertz; Patrick Corrigan; Joel and Sharon Harris; Lance Lekander; Elizabeth Rosen; Kate Sweeney; Sam Ward, Nicole Wong, Escletxa.

Photography Credits: iv (cl) Photodisc/Getty Images; iv (bc) ©Corbis Royalty Free; iv (bl) Corbis Royalty Free; iv (b) Getty Images/PhotoDisc; v (b) Getty Images; vi ©Douglas Peebles Photography/Alamy; vi (br) ©G. K. & Vikki Hart /PhotoDisc/Getty Images; vii (tr) ©Digital Vision/Getty Images; vii (t) Getty Images; viii NPS Photo by Peter Jones; viii (bl) ©Photodisc/Getty Images; viii (t) ©Corbis; ix (tr) Corbis; ix (bl) ©PhotoDisc/Getty Images; ix (bl) Corbis; 2 ©Tony Gable and C Squared Studios/Getty Images; 2 (bl) Jens Hilberger/Fotolia; 2 (br) © C Squared Studios/ PhotoDisc/Getty Images; 2 (bc) Artville / Getty Images; 3 Brand X Pictures/Getty Images; 3 (br) ©Jason Edwards/National Geographic/Getty Images; 3 (tl) ©Philip Coblentz/Brand X PicturesGetty Images; 4 (bl) ©Comstock / Getty Images; 4 (cl) ©Douglas Peebles Photography/Alamy; 5 (t) ©GK & Vikki Hart/Photodisc/Getty Images; 5 (cr) ©Corbis Royalty Free; 6 (c) ©Photos.com/Jupiterimages/Getty Images; 6 Corbis; 8 (tr) Getty Images/PhotoDisc; 8 (tl) © Corbis/Royalty Free; 8 (tc) ©PhotoDisc/Getty Images; 8 (c) ©PhotoDisc/Getty Images; 8 (br) Getty Images/DAJ; 8 C. Sherburne/PhotoLink/Getty Images/PhotoDisc; 8 (cr) AGE Fotostock; 8 (c) Corbis/Royalty Free; 9 Corbis/Royalty Free; 9 Corbis; 9 Corbis; 9 Getty Images Royalty Free; 9 Joseph Sohm-Visions of America/Getty Images/Digital Vision; 9 Corbis/Royalty Free; 16 Library of Congress; 17 (tr) ©Bridgeman Art Library/American Photographer/Getty Images; 18 (bl) ©rangizzz/Shutterstock; 18 (br) Polka Dot Images/Jupiterimages/Getty Images; 18 (tl) © PhotoDisc/Getty Images; 18 (tl) ©Comstock/Getty Images; 18 (bl) ©rangizzz/Shutterstock; 19 (tl) ©Comstock/Getty Images; 19 (br) ©Creatas/Jupiterimages/Getty Images; 20 (c) ©Photos.com/Jupiterimages/Getty Images; 21 (b) ©Catherine Karnow/Corbis; 21 (t) ©Peter Turnley/Corbis; 22 (b) ©Comstock/Getty Images; 22 (t) Corbis; 23 (b) ©Reuters NewMedia/Corbis; 26 Corbis; 27 (tl) ©Herbert Cosby/ Alamy; 27 (t) Stockbyte/Getty Images; 27 (tr) ©Corbis; 28 (tr) ©Digital Vision/Getty Images; 29 (t) ©Alamy; 30 (t) ©Comstock Images/Getty Images; 30 ©Houghton Mifflin Harcourt; 31 (b) Stockdisc/Getty Images; 36 ©Ellen McKnight/Alamy Images; 37 Image100/Alamy; 38 ©Digital Vision/Getty Images; 38 (t) ©ludmilafoto/Shutterstock; 39 © Visions of America, LLC / Alamy; 39 ©C Squared Studios/Getty Images; 40 (b) ©Nigel Pavitt/Getty Images; 40 ©Tony Gable and C Squared Studios/Getty Images; 40 ©Tony Gable and C Squared Studios/Photo Disc/Getty Images; 46 ©Science Source/Getty Images; 47 (tl) ©Stringer/Getty Images; 47 (t) ©Bettmann/Corbis; 47 (t) ©Brooks Kraft/Sygma/Corbis; 47 (t) ©Jaguar PS/Shutterstock; 47 (t) ©Steve Lipofsky/Corbis; 47 (tl) Comstock/Getty Images; 49 (t) Stockbyte/Getty Images; 49 (t) ©Comstock Images/Getty Images; 49 ©Houghton Mifflin Harcourt; 50 (tr) ©Corbis; 50 ©Visions of America, LLC / Alamy; 50 (c) Corbis/Royalty Free; 50 (tc) Getty Images; 50 (cr) Corbis/Royalty Free; 51 (b) Brand X Pictures/Getty Images; 52 (c) ©Katrina Brown/Fotolia; 52 (b) Getty Images Royalty Free; 52 (cr) © Digital Vision/Getty Images; 52 ©Digital Vision/Getty Images; 54 (cr) PhotoDisc / Getty Images; 55 ©Robert Glusic/Photodisc/Getty Images; 55 Digital Vision / Getty Images; 55 ©Photodisc/Getty Images; 55 (b) Getty Images/Photodisc; 64 (bl) Comstock Images/Jupiterimages/Getty Images; 64 (bl) ©rangizzz/Shutterstock; 64 (tl) ©PhotoDisc/ Getty Royalty Free; 65 (l) ©Houghton Mifflin Harcourt; 66 (br) ©Imagebroker/Alamy Images; 66 (cr) ©Getty Images; 66 ©Photodisc/Getty Images; 67 (bl) ©Katrina Brown/Fotolia; 67 (tr) © Digital Vision/Getty Images; 67 (cr) ©Getty Images; 67